How to SURVIVE *When You* LOST ALL HOPE

HOW TO OVERCOME
Depression, Anxiety, Fear, Addiction AND *Suicidal Thought*

BISHOP ISAAC OGBETA

outskirts press

THIS BOOK IS DEDICATED TO CHARITY THE MARTYR:
The most courageous and Lovely person who ever lived on
the surface of the earth is called CHARITY: The people reply, "Who would have believed what we now report? Who
could have seen the Lord's hand in this? It was the will of the
Lord that his servants grow like a plant taking roots in dry
ground. He had no dignity or beauty to make us take notice
of him. There was nothing attractive about him, nothing that
would draw us to him. We despised him and rejected him;
he endured suffering and pain. No one would even look at
him—we ignored as if he were nothing. But he endured the
suffering that should have been ours, the pain that we should
have borne.

All the while we thought that his suffering was the punishment sent by God. But because of our sins he was wounded,
beaten because of the evil we did. We are healed by the punishment he suffered, made whole by the blows he received.
All of us were like sheep that were lost, each of us going his
own way; But the Lord made the punishment fall on him, the
punishment all of us deserved. He was treated harshly but
endured it humbly; he never said a word. Like a lamb about
to be slaughtered, like a sheep about to be sheared, he never
said a word. He was arrested and sentenced and led off to
die, and no one cared about his fate. He was put to death by
the sins of our people. He was placed in a grave with those
who are evil; he was buried with the rich, even though he
had never committed a crime or ever told a lie. The Lord says
it was my will that he should suffer; his death was a sacrifice
to bring forgiveness. And so, he will see his descendants; he
will live along life, and through him my purpose will succeed.
After a life of suffering, he will again have joy; he will know

that he did not suffer in vain. My devoted servant, with whom I am well pleased, will bear the punishment of many and for his sake I will forgive them. And so, I will give him a place of honor, a place among the great and powerful. He willingly gave his life and shared the fate of evil men. He took the place of many sinners and prayed that they might be forgiven.

Table of Contents

Foreword

BY CHARITY THE MARTYR:

THE MOST COURAGOUES AND LOVELY PERSON WHO EVER LIVED ON THE SURFACE OF THE EARTH: KNOWING THAT YOUR LIFE HERE ON EARTH IS NOT PERMANENT: THEREFORE LOVE AND HELP OTHERS: HELP ORPHANS, THE WIDOW, THE FATHERLESS, THE DIRVORCED, THE SINGLE,THE LESS PREVILAGE, THE HUNGRY, THE HOMELESS, THE PRISONERS, THE CAPTIVE, THE SICK,THE OUTCAST, THE REJECTED, THE DOWNTRODDEN, THE POOR, THE LOST , THE LONELY, THE STRANGERS, THE WEAK, THE REFUGEES, THE HEART-BROKEN: THE ONLY REASON WHY YOU ARE HERE ON EARTH TO FULFILL A PURPOSE; GOD'S PURPOSE AND TO LEAVE YOUR LEGECY BEHIND; I PRAY THAT THIS BOOK WILL BE A BLESSING TO YOUR LIFE IN JESUS NAME. AMEN:

IN MEMORY OF CHARITY: CONTINUE READING.......

Introduction

**WHAT IS THE BEST WAY TO GET OUT OF
DEPRESSION, WHEN YOU HAVE LOST ALL
HOPE AND BECOME EXTREMELY LONELY
AND LIFE IS MEANINGLESS TO YOU.**

What is the meaning of Depression?

Depression is a state of low mood and aversion to activity. It can affect a person's thoughts, behavior, motivation, feelings, and sense of well-being. It may feature sadness, difficulty in thinking and concentration and a significant increase/decrease in appetite and time spent sleeping, and people experiencing depression may have feelings of dejection, hopelessness, and sometimes, suicidal thoughts. It can either be short term or long term. Depressed mood is a symptom of some mood disorders such as major depressive disorder or dysthymia; It is a normal temporary reaction to life events, such as the loss of a loved one; and it is also a symptom of some physical diseases and a side effect of some drugs and medical treatments. (major depressive disorder) is a common and serious medical illness that negatively affects how you feel, the way you think and how you act; Depression causes feelings of sadness and/or a loss of interest in activities once enjoyed; Feeling sad or having a depressed mood; Feelings of severe despondency and dejection; melancholy; misery; sadness; unhappiness; sorrow; woe; gloom; desolation; discouragement; hopelessness; despair.

Are you struggling emotionally or mentally and going through a similar situation of depression and lost all hope recently? Are you in depression? Lost all hope, are you in kind of extreme loneliness, and feels no one cares for you or feel abandon, rejected, abused, betrayed and suicidal?

When some people find themselves in this situation of Depression and losing all hope, some people want to get out of this situation of depression and lost of all hope by resulting to taking drugs or alcohol or medication which affect them emotionally and mentally and in so doing become addicted and even make the matter worse and some are now suffering from addiction which may result in uncontrollable and criminal behavior of violence and imprisonment and even death.

WHAT IS THE CAUSE OF DEPRESSION AND ANXIETY?

The answer is Excessive stress brings you deeper into depression and Anxiety.

HOW STRESS WORKS IN OUR BODY?

When the brain perceives a danger or a stressful situation, it activates fight or flight response system by releasing some specific hormones, which prepares the body to release excessive energy to either fight or flight from the situation.

The fight or flight system was designed by the nature to protect us from actual dangerous or life-threatening situations. However, some people have a very sensitive warning systems which triggers fight and flight activation in the very small stressful and non-life-threatening events such as having an argument with a boss or spouse, missing a deadline of an office report, arriving late to the office, or other household financial emergencies. This hypersensitivity increases the frequency of the activation of fight or flight mode by implementing the rapid discharge of stress hormones in the body which result in many negative impacts on both the body and mind.

What is the solution?

Anti-depression medication only gives you a short-term relief. Meditation is the best way to overcome from depression because meditation works in equal and opposite way that stress does.

When we meditate our mind, feel calm, and release happiness hormones such as serotonin, which creates a sense of happiness and boosts our mood. Some studies have shown that meditation shrinks the part of the brain that controls anxiety and fear. Less anxiety and fear translate to less stress. Less stress means more joy.

And also, the best way to get out of depression; Self-acceptance is one of the best way: We fall in this pit of sadness because we lose faith from us due to mere awful situations of life. Accept what is happening, accept what you are, accept the outcome, accept the betrayal. This acceptance would be difficult but you cannot run from it. Find that one way which can make you express your emotions by prayers and meditations, reading the bible, exercise, writing, cooking, outing, going with friends to social events, going to religious gathering, watching good encouraging videos, playing, vising the sick in the hospital to pray for them and visiting the prison to pray for them, volunteer your time to feed the homeless and the hungry; You don't need to be expert in that, just do it for the sake of feeling pleasure. Unleash all what you have packed in yourself as burden in form of activity and trust me you will feel great about yourself and donate for a good course and be involve in charitable work and call on pastors or rabbi to pray for you and if you cannot find the organization to be involve with you can visit the websites;

www.worldwiderelieforganization.org or for words of encouragement or prayers email; bishopisaacogbeta@gmail.com

1. **Lost all hopes?** Losing hope is such a pain that all the other physical pain seems totally like nothing. I can feel how hard it is to tolerate the MENTAL TORTURE IN COMPARISION TO PHYSICAL WOUND. No matter what age you are hope can never be shattered or lost. Start afresh from now just sit and think about yourself in which direction you w3ant to walk. If needed, discuss it with someone whom you feel can guide ask freely. Hopeless life cannot lead you anywhere. Create a plan but don't blindly stick to it. Give your honest efforts and wait for the best results meanwhile don't lose hope please; I will encourage you to read the book of Matthew chapter 6 verses 25-33 and Philippians chapter 4 verses 6-7

ADDICTION is when the body or mind badly needs something in order to work right. is a psychological and physical inability to stop consuming a chemical, drug, activity or substance even though it is causing psychological harm.

The term addiction does not only refer to dependence on substance such as heroin or cocaine. A person who cannot stop taking a particular drug or chemical has a substance dependence.

Some addictions also involve an inability to stop partaking in activities, such as gambling, eating, or working. In these circumstances, a person has a behavioral addiction.

Addiction is a chronic disease that can also result from taking medications. The overuse of prescribed opioid painkillers, for example, causes 115 deaths every day in United States.

When a person experiences addiction, they cannot control how they use or partake in an activity, and they become dependent on it to cope with daily life.

Every year, addiction to alcohol, tobacco, illicit drugs, and prescription opioids costs the United States economy upward of $740 billion in treatment costs, lost work, and the effect of crime.

Most people start using d a drug or first engage in an activity voluntarily. However, addiction can take over and reduce self-control.

WHAT ARE THE UNDERLYING CAUSES
OF DRUG ADDICTION?

Drug addiction is a compulsive and chronic disorder of the mind that leads an individual to habitually use of substance in an effort to achieve a desired outcome from it. —often the trademark high.

Across America, around 20 million people who needed substance abuse treatment in 2013 didn't receive it, according to the Substance Abuse and Mental Health Services Administration. Over time, the outcome the addict is seeking may change. For instance, initial experimentation with a drug is often rooted in curiosity. As use of the substance becomes more frequent, the body start to grow physically dependent on the drugs in order to function properly.

Signs of addiction include tolerance, a loss of control over how much or how often you use, an obsession with the substance, abandoning events and activities you used to enjoy, and continuing to use drugs even though they have negative effects on your life.

Anyone who begins to experience symptoms of withdrawal –whether mild or severe—in the absence of the substance, is likely dependent on the substance. Withdrawal symptoms can vary from drug to drug and include;

- Trembling,
- Fatigue
- Anxiety
- Depression
- Nausea, with or without vomiting

- Excessive perspiration
- Headache
- Insomnia.

WHY DO PEOPLE USE DRUGS?

For many people, drug use starts with mere experimentation. This can stem from curiosity about what is like to be high or peer pressure.

Others stumble upon drugs as an escape from the uncomfortable feelings of sadness or anxiety they experience.

The Anxiety and Depression Association of America report about 20 percent of substance abusers have an anxiety disorder or mood disorder, such as depression. When someone is struggle with mental illness, it often isn't visible to the sufferer, who is in the thick of it.

For many Americans, drug use starts with a prescription. Opiate-based drugs like OxyContin are notorious for both their addictive properties and their likelihood of being over-prescribed. The Los Angeles Times reported more around 92,200 people were treated for overdoses on prescription opioid pain relievers in 2010. The Centers for Disease Control and Prevention notes astounding 259 million prescriptions were written for opioid painkillers in 2012.

There are individuals who are given prescriptions they are very much in need of, such patient with anxiety who is given a script for benzodiazepines. These drugs are highly addictive, and as a result they should only be prescribed for short periods of time. In fact, Help guide States that individuals who take prescribed benzos for a couple months or longer will very likely become addicted to them, noting that the anti-anxiety therapeutic qualities of the drug will lose their efficacy after four to six months' time.

WHAT ARE THEY USING?

The most common abused substance in America is alcohol. Across the country, the National Council on Alcoholism and Drug Dependence, Inc States that 17.6 million adults are either dependent on or abusing alcohol. When it comes to drugs, no one drug is abused more than marijuana. Other drugs that often lead to addiction include;

- Prescription opioid pain relievers, such as hydrocodone
- Cocaine
- Heroin
- Prescription benzodiazepines
- Spice
- Barbiturates, like phenobarbital

TREATMENT

According to a review, in order to be effective, all pharmacological or biologically based treatments for addiction need to be integrated into other established forms of addiction rehabilitation, such as cognitive behavioral therapy, individual and group psychotherapy, behavior-modification strategies, twelve-steps programs, and residential treatment.

BEHAVOIRAL THERAPY; A meta-analytic review on the efficacy of various behavioral therapies

ANXIETY is an emotion characterized by an unpleasant state of inner turmoil, often, accompanied by nervous behavior such as the pacing back and forth, somatic complaints and rumination. It is the subjectively unpleasant feelings of dread over anticipated events, such as the feelings of imminent death. Anxiety is not the same as fear, which is a response to a real or perceived immediate threat, whereas anxiety involves the expectation of future threat. Anxiety is a feeling of uneasiness and worry, usually generalized and unfocused as an overreaction to a situation that is only subjectively seen as menacing. It is often accompanied by muscular tension, restlessness fatigue and problems in concentration. Anxiety can be appropriate, but when experienced regularly the individual may suffer from an anxiety disorder.

People facing anxiety may withdraw from situations which have provoked anxiety in the past. There are various types of anxiety. Existential anxiety can occur when a person faces angst, an existential crisis, or nihilistic feelings. People can also face mathematical anxiety, somatic anxiety, stage fright, or test anxiety. Social anxiety and strange anxiety are caused when people are apprehensive around strangers or other people in general. A nervous disorder characterized by a state of excessive uneasiness and apprehension, typically with compulsive behavior or panic attacks; a feeling of worry, nervousness, or unease, typically about an imminent event or something with an uncertain outcome; worry; concern; apprehension;

consternation; uneasiness; perturbation; trepidation; tension; fear; impatience; yearning; foreboding; agitation;

SUICIDE; from Latin word suicidium, is the act of taking one's own life. Attempted suicide or non-fatal suicidal behavior is self-injury with the desire to end one's life that does not result in death. Assisted suicide is when one individual helps another bring about their own death indirectly via providing either advice or the means to the end. This is in contrast to euthanasia, where another person takes a more active role in bringing about a person's death. Suicidal ideation is thoughts of ending one's life but not taking any active efforts to do so. In a murder-suicide (or homicide-suicide) the individual aims at taking the life of others at the same time. A special case of this is extended suicide, where the murder is motivated by seeing the murdered persons an extension of their self. Opponents of commit argue that it implies that suicide is a criminal, sinful, or morally wrong.

SUICIDE IS THE ACT OF INTENTIONALLY CAUSING ONE'S OWN DEATH; THE ACT OF KILLING YOURSELF INTENTIONALLY, OR CAUSING ANOTHER PEOPLES DEATH

Mental disorders, including depression, bipolar disorder, schizophrenia, personality disorders, anxiety disorders, and substance abuse—including alcoholism and the use of benzodiazepines—are risk factors. Some suicides are impulsive acts due to stress, such as from financial difficulties, troubles with relationships, or bullying. Those who have previously attempted suicide are at a higher risk for the future attempts. Effective suicide prevention efforts include limiting access to methods of suicide—such as firearms, drugs and poisons; treating mental disorder and substance misuse; proper media reporting of suicide; and improving economic conditions. Even though crisis hotlines are common, there is a little evidence of their effectiveness.

CAUSES; Hanging, pesticide poisoning, firearms.

RISK FACTORS; Factors that affect the risk of suicide include mental disorders, drug misuse, psychological states, cultural family and social situations and genetics. Mental disorders and substance misuse frequently co-exist. Other risk factors include having previously attempted suicide, the ready availability of a means to take one's own life, a family history of suicide, or the presence of traumatic brain injury. For example, suicide rates have been found to be greater in households with firearms than those without them.

SOCIO-ECONOMIC PROBLEMS; such as unemployment, poverty, homelessness, and discrimination may trigger suicidal thoughts. About 15-40 % of people leave a suicide note. War veterans have higher risk of suicide due in part to higher rates of mental illness such as post traumatic stress disorder and physical health problems related to war. Genetics appears to account for between 38% and 55% of suicidal behaviors. Suicide may also occur as a local cluster of cases.

Depression, bipolar disorder, schizophrenia, personality disorders, anxiety disorders, alcoholism, substance abuse.

PREVENTION; Suicide prevention is a term used for the collective efforts to reduce the incidence of suicide through preventative measures. Reducing access to certain methods, such as firearms or toxins such as opioids can reduce risk. Other measures include reducing access to charcoal (for burning) and adding barriers on bridges and subways platforms. Treatment of drug and alcohol addiction, depression, and those who have attempted suicide in the past may also be effective. Some have proposed reducing access to alcohol as a preventative strategy (such as reducing the numbers of bars). Although crisis hotlines are common there is little evidence to support or to refute their effectiveness.

In young adults who have recently thought about suicide, cognitive behavioral therapy appears to improve outcomes. Economics developments through its ability to reduce poverty may be able to decrease suicide rates. Efforts to increase social connection, especially in elderly males, may be effective. The World Suicide Prevention Day is observed annually on September 10 with the support of International Association for Suicide Prevention and the World Health Organization. Preventing childhood trauma provides an opportunity for suicide Prevention.

CHILDHOOD TRAUMA; Childhood trauma is a risk factor for suicidality. Some may take their own lives to escape bullying or prejudice. A history of childhood sexual abuse. And time spent in foster care are also risk factors. Sexual abuse is believed to contribute approximately 20% of all the overall risk.

PROBLEMS IN GAMBLING; Problems gambling is associated with increased suicidal ideation and attempts compared to the general population.', between 12 and 24% pathological gamblers attempt suicide. The rate of suicide among their spouses is three times greater than that of the general population. Other factors that increase the risk in problems gamblers include mental illness, alcohol and drug abuse.

SUBSTANCE MISUSE; Substance misuse is the second most common risk factor for suicide after major depression and bipolar disorder. Both chronic substance misuse as well as acute intoxication are associated. When combined with personal grief, such bereavement, the risk is further increased. Substance misuse is also associated with mental health disorders.

Most people are under the influence of sedative-hypnotic drugs (such as alcohol or benzodiazepines) when they die by suicide with alcoholism present in between 15 and 61% of cases. Use of prescribed benzodiazepines is associated with an increased rate of attempted and committed suicide. The presuicidal effects of benzodiazepines are suspected to be due to a psychiatric disturbance caused by side effects or withdrawal symptoms.

Alcoholics who attempt suicide are usually male, older, and have tried to take their own lives in the past. Between 3 and 35% of deaths among those who use heroin are due to suicide (approximately fourteenfold greater than those who do not use). In adolescents who misuse alcohol, neurological and psychological dysfunctions may contribute to the increased risk of suicide.

The misuse of cocaine and methamphetamine has a high

correlation with suicide. In those who use cocaine the risk is greatest during the withdrawal phase. Those who used inhalants are also at significant risk with around 20% attempting suicide at some point and more than 65% considering it. Smoking cigarettes is associated with risk of suicide.

MEDICAL CONDITIONS; There is an association between suicidality and physical health problems such as chronic pain, traumatic brain injury, cancer, kidney failure (requiring hemodialysis), HIV, and systemic lupus erythematosus. The diagnosis of cancer approximately doubles the subsequent frequency of suicide. The prevalence of increased suicidality persisted after adjusting for depressive illness and alcohol abuse. Among people with more than one medical condition the frequency was particularly high. In Japan, health problems are listed as the primary justification for suicide.

Sleep disturbances such as insomnia and sleep apnea are risk factors for depression and suicide. In some instances, the sleep disturbances may be a risk factor independent of depression. A number of other medical conditions may present with symptoms similar to mood disorders, including hypothyroidism, Alzheimer's, brain tumors.

PSYCHSOCIAL STATES; A number of psychological states increase the risk of suicide including; hopelessness, loss of pleasure in life, depression and anxiousness. A poor ability to solve problems', the loss of abilities one used to have, and poor impulse control also played a role. In older adults the perception of being a burden to others is important. Suicide in which the reason is that the person feels that they are not part of society is known as egoistic suicide. Rates of suicide appear to decrease around Christmas. One study however found the risk may be greater for males on their birthday. In those who are admitted to hospital, agitation appears to be a risk.

Recent life stresses such as a loss of a family member or friend, loss of a job, or social isolation (such as living alone) increase the risk. Those who have never married are also at greater risk. Being religious may reduce one's risk of suicide well beliefs that suicide is noble may increase it. This has been attributed to the negative stance many religious takes against suicide and to the greater connectedness religion may give.

POVERTY; Poverty is associated with the risk of suicide. Increasing relative poverty compared to those around a person increases suicide risk. Over 200,000 farmers in India have died by suicide since 1997, partly due to issues of debt. In China is three times as likely in rural regions as urban ones, partly it is believed, due to financial difficulties in this area of the country.

THE MEDIA, including the internet has also contributed into committing of suicide by those who bully others in the internet.

10 SIGNS OF SUICIDE THAT COULD HELP YOU DETERMINE IF SOMEONE IS SUICIDAL.

- Threatening to hurt or kill himself or herself.
- Looking for ways to kill himself or herself.
- Talking or writing about death, dying or suicide.

- Rage, anger, seeking revenge.
- Feeling trapped, like there is no way out.
- Increasing alcohol or drug use.
- Withdrawing from friends, family or society.
- Anxiety, agitation, unable to sleep or sleeping all the time.
- Dramatic changes in mood.
- No reason for living, no sense of purpose in life.

Limiting access to methods of suicide, treating mental disorders and substance misuse, proper media reporting of suicide, improving economic conditions. Three quarters of suicides globally occur in low and middle-income countries. Europe had the highest rates of suicide by region. There are estimated 10-20 million non-fatal attempted suicides every year. Non- fatal suicide attempts may lead to injury and long-term disabilities. In the Western World, attempts are more common among young people and among females.

Views on suicide have been influenced by broad existential themes such as religion, honor, and the meaning of life. The Abrahamic religions traditionally consider suicide as an offence towards God, due to the belief in the sanctity of life. During the samurai era in Japan, a form of suicide known as seppuku (hara-kiri) was respected as a means of making up for failure or as a form of protest. Sati, a practice outlawed by the British Raj, expected the India widow to kill herself on her husband's funeral fire, either willingly or under pressure from her family and society. Suicide and attempted suicide, while previously illegal, are no longer so in most Western countries, it remains a criminal offense in many countries. In the 20th and 21st centuries, suicide has been used on rare occasions as form of protest, and kamikaze and suicide bombings have been used as a military or terrorist tactic.

HOW TO OVERCOME DEPPRESSION; ANXIETY; FEAR; ADDICTION, DESPAIR AND SUICIDE; FACING CHALLENGES, YOU CAN OVERCOME

First; What is the definition of Hope? Hope means a feeling of expectation and a desire for certain thing to come: a feeling of expectation that something good is going to happen or something good is coming;

A person or thing that may help or save someone; A desire accompanied by expectation or expectation of fulfillment or success; Aspiration; desire wish; expectation; ambition; aim; goal; conviction; assurance; optimism; dream;

A ground for believing that something good may happen; trust; Confidence; belief; promise; possibility.

But the Hope I want to talk about is not the worldly hope of wishful thinking; for example; I hope my team wins the Super Bowl, or I hope I get a raise. but I am speaking of the spiritual hope or biblical hope which is far greater than the worldly hope; Biblical hope is not a hope-so but it is a known-so; HOPE IS NOT A FEELING OR EMOTION. HOPE IS THE KNOWLEDGE OF FACTS. A biblical definition of hope is far superior to that of the world. Instead of wishing or hoping for something to happen, a believer knows that their hope is SOLID, CONTRETE EVIDENCE because it is GROUNDED

IN THE WORD OF GOD AND WE KNOW THAT GOD CANNOT LIE; Hebrew 6:18 Numbers 23:19.

The bible definition of Faith as "**assurance of things** hoped for, **the conviction of things not seen.** (Hebrew 11:1) It is a hope that like faith---a faith that cannot be moved by circumstances or what the eyes can see because an unseen God is seen in his faithfulness.

Romans 8:24-25 where the bible tells the believer; "FOR IN THIS HOPE WE WERE SAVED. NOW HOPE THAT IS SEEN IS NOT HOPE; FOR WHO HOPES FOR WHAT IS SEES? BUT IF WE HOPE FOR WHAT WE DO NOT SEE, WE WAIT FOR IT WITH PATIENCE.

2 Corinthians 5:7 says FOR WE LIVE BY FAITH NOT BY SIGHT.

2 Corinthians 4:18 says SO WE FIX OUR EYES NOT ON WHAT IS SEEN, BUT ON WHAT IS UNSEEN, SINCE WHAT IS SEEN IS TEMPORARY, BUT WHAT IS UNSEEN IS ETERNAL (NIV)

SO, WE DON'T LOOK AT THE TROUBLES WE CAN SEE NOW; RATHER, WE FIX OUR EYES ON THINGS THAT WHICH CANNOT BE SEEN. FOR THE THINGS WE SEE NOW WILL SOON BE GONE, BUT THE THINGS WE CANNOT SEE WILL LAST FOREVER. (NLT)

ALL THESE SMALL AND TEMPORARY TROUBLE WE SUFFER WILL BRING US A TREMENDOUS AND ETERNAL GLORY,

MUCH GREATER THAN THE TROUBLE. FOR WE FIX OUR ATTENTION, NOT ON THINGS THAT ARE SEEN, BUT ON THINGS THAT ARE NOT SEEN. WHAT CAN BE SEEN LASTS ONLY FOR A TIME, BUT WHAT CANNOT BE SEEN LASTS FOREVER. 2 Corinthians 4:17-18 (GNT)

Hope is the life force that keeps us going and gives us something to live for. Hope is a crucial part of dealing with life's problems and maintain resilience in the face of obstacles and opposition. Even a glimmer of hope that our situation will turn around can keep us going.

Though, when we begin to lose hope, things can seem bleak. When we run into constant resistance and are prevented from reaching our goals we can begin to feel like there is nothing to live for. If we cannot get to where we want to be and don't feel in control of our lives, what is the point? If you or someone else is feeling apathetic and are tired of running the rat race of life you may be starting to lose hope. In order to open up new and fulfilling possibilities for your future, you may need to nurture hope.

CHAPTER 1

You Need Faith, Courage, Resilience, Persistence

Faith is the Confidence in What We Hope for and Assurance About What We Do Not See

FAITH means believing the unbelievable

Hope means hoping when everything seems hopeless

The root of suicidal thought comes from when a person thought he had lost all hope and had been through many failures on many fronts in a short period of time, causing an immense amount of pain. For example, I have failed in marriages, business, and life in general; In life, sometimes we feel lost and broken, We feel all hope is gone and we think that we have no reason to live anymore; because I am in debt, my wife /husband left me, someone close relatives died, I am unemployed, I am lonely or I am a failure, I am going through separation or going through bitter divorced or fighting for the custody of my children and depressed and worries ;sometimes you find it difficult to get out of bed in the mooring; And life seems to put you in the wilderness all alone by yourself and it seems that nobody understand you and nobody cares. You don't feel like going on because you have lost all strength and hope.t is a lie; It signal the beginning of the end.

Anytime we suffer immense amounts of failure and defeat, we lose much of the hope we have. Like will power hope is easily drained and depleted. When all you can do is worry, stress, and contemplate your greatest fears, after a major failure it is easy to lose hope. If you have suffered through some major calamities and strife recently, and feel like you have lost all hope, is not true.

There is hope even when a tree had been cut down; it can come back to life and sprout. Even though its roots grow old and its stump dies in the ground, with water it's sprout like a young plant. Even any seed planted must die before it grows to become a tree. Those situations are setting you up for a life far greater and brighter; It may not seem like it right now, but overtime, the truth will be illuminated;

But the question remains what do when it seems that the whole world around you are collapsing or everything around you come crashing down. life is like a camera lens' What you choose to focus in becomes clearer and more real to us. When you focus on the negatives then you become more depressed and become hopeless but when you focus on the positives then you become hopeful and good things are seen.

Assume, you have a car. If it breaks down, normally you take it to somebody the mechanic to fix it. But you don't pour acid on it, or blow it up or drive it over the cliff. It is a broken car and broken things can be fixed or repaired. Therefore, if anything is broken in your life emotionally, physically or mentally or Spiritually it can be fixed by the mechanic who created your life and your body(God): If you are sick physically you go to see the doctor; So, if your issues are not physical but emotional because sickness you can see with your eyes are not different than the sickness you cannot see with your eyes is called mind sickness or emotional trauma which can be cured. The illness physically or emotionally can be treated; The problem or the issue therefore is that you don't believe you can be treated or you don't know how. Both can be addressed or treated. People that are suicidal always feeling lonely, isolated, depressed, and hopeless. But I challenge you as you read this book that there is hope for your future no matter what situation you are going through at this very moment.

God who brings the dead to life and brings into existence what does not exist will resurrect your dead situation back to life. Roman 4:17

ONLY BELIEVE; ONLY BELIEVE ONLY; ONLY BELIEVE

AGAINST ALL HOPE, ABRAHAM BELIEVED IN HOPE; Roman 4;18

Abraham believed and hoped, even when there no reason for hoping, and so became the father of many nations. "Just as the Scriptures says, "Your descendants will be as many as the stars."

He was then almost one hundred years old, but his faith did not weaken, when he thought of his body, which was already practically dead, or of the fact that Sarah could not have children. His faith did not leave him, or he did not doubt God promise; his faith filled him with power and gave praise to God. He was absolutely sure that God would be able to do what he has promised. That is why Abraham through faith, was accepted as righteous by God. The words "he was accepted as righteous were not written for him alone.by God. They were also written for us who were to be accepted as righteous, who believe in him who raised Jesus our Lord from the death. Because of our sins he was given over to die, and he was raised from dead in order to put us right with God.

THE LAMENTATION OF JOB;

JOB LAMENTED WHEN HE LOST ALL HOPE; BUT JOB DID NOT COMMIT SUICIDE BECAUSE THERE IS STILL HOPE EVEN WHEN YOU HAVE LOST ALL HOPE; Job chapter 3

JOB COMPLAINT TO GOD; Finally, Job broke the silence and cursed the day on which he had been born. O God, put a curse on the day I was born; put a curse on the night when I was conceived. Turn that day into darkness, God never again remember that day; never again let light shine on it. Make it a day of gloom and thick darkness, cover it with clouds, and blot out the sun. Blot that night out of the year, and never let it be counted again; make it a barren, a joyless night. Tell the sorcerers to curse that day, those who knows how to control Leviathan. Keep the morning star from shinning; give that night no hope of dawn. Curse that night for letting me be born, for exposing me to trouble and grief. I wish I had died in my mother's womb or died the moment I was born. Why did my mother hold me on her knees? Why did she feed me at her breast? If I had died then I would be at rest now, sleeping like the kings and rulers who rebuilt ancient palaces.

Then I would be sleeping like princes who filled their houses with gold and silver or sleeping like stillborn child. In the grave wicked people stops their evil, and tired workers find rest at last. Even prisoners enjoy peace, free from shouts and harsh commands. Everyone is there the famous and the unknown, and slaves at last are free. Why let people go on living in misery? Why give light to those in grief? They wait for death but it never comes; they prefer a grave than any treasure. They are not happy till they are dead and buried; God keep their future hidden and hems them in on every side. Instead of eating I mourn, and I cannot stop groaning. Everything I fear and dread comes true. I have no peace; no rest and my troubles never end.

WHERE DO I FIND HOPE WHEN MY LIFE IS FALLING APART?

Is your life falling apart? Are you or someone you know feeling discouraged and depressed, like nothing working out? May be your marriage is falling apart or you lost your job. Where do you go for hope?

The world will tell you that if only you just find the right person to be with then you will find hope. Or you just get a new job, you will find hope. Or if you have some more money, you will find hope. But all those things can never satisfy.

But there something—someone—who can. Today, Jesus says to you, "Come into me all you that labor and are heavy-laden, and I will give you rest" Matthew 11:28; If you are feeling stressed out and overwhelmed, and you feeling falling apart and you cannot go on for another day Jesus says he will bring rest to your soul. Psalms 34:17-18 says "The righteous cry out, and the Lord hears them; he delivers them from all their troubles. The Lord is close to the broken-hearted saves those who are crushed in spirit. In the Good News Translation, it says "The Lord is near to those who are discouraged; and he saves those who have lost all hope."

I will advise you to read Psalms 107 if you going through hopelessness situation and when you ask this question What strength do I have to keep on living? Why go on living when I have no hope?

If your hopelessness is critical and is gone out of hand and it seems you have lost all hope

Then read everything below and try to memorize them

God alone knows the plans he has for you, plans to bring you prosperity and not disaster, plans to bring about the future you hope for. Book of Jeremiah 29:11

Why am I so sad? Why am I so troubled? I will put my hope in God, and once again I will praise him, my savoir and my God. Psalms 42:11

But those who trust in the Lord for help, will find their strength renewed. They will rise on wings like eagles; They will run and not get weary; they will walk and not grow weak. Isaiah 41:31

The Lord will protect you from all danger; he will keep you safe. He will protect you as you come and go now and forever. Psalms 121:7-8

May God, the source of hope, fill you with all joy and peace by means of your faith in him, so that your hope will continue to grow by the power of the Holy Spirit. Roman 15:13

To have faith is to be sure of the things we hope for, to be certain of things we cannot see. Hebrew 11:1

When I was a child, my speech, feelings, and thinking were all those of a child; now that I am an adult, I have no more use for childish ways. What we see now is like a dim image in a mirror; then we shall see face to face. What I know now is only partial; then it will be complete—as complete as Gods knowledge of me. Meanwhile these three remain: faith, hope and love; and the greatest of these is love. 1 Corinthians 13:11-13

Come to me, all of you who are tired from carrying heavy loads, I will give you rest Matthew 11:28

1 Peter 4:12-19 says

My dear friends, do not be surprised at the painful test you are suffering, as though something unusual were happening to you. Rather be glad that you are sharing Christ's sufferings, so that you may be full of joy when his glory is revealed. Happy are you if you are insulted because you are Christ followers; this means that the glorious spirit, the spirit of God, is resting on you. However, if you suffer because you are a Christian, don't be ashamed of it, but thank God that you bear Christ name.

The time has come for judgment to begin, and God's own people are the first to be judged. If it starts with us, how will it end with those who do not believe the Good News from God? As the Scriptures says' It is difficult for good people to be saved; What, then, will become of godless sinners? So then, those who suffer because it is will for them, should by their good actions trust themselves completely to their Creator, who always keeps his promise

I consider that what we suffer at this present time cannot be compared at all with the glory that is going to be revealed to us.

All of creation waits with eager longing for God to reveal his children. **For creation was condemned to lose its purpose, not of his own will, but because God willed it to be so.**

Yet there was the hope that creation itself would one day be set free from slavery to decay and would share the glorious freedom of the children of God. **For we know that up to the present time all of creation groans with pain, like the pain of childbirth**. But it is not just creation alone which groans; we who have the spirit as the first of God's gifts also groans within ourselves as we wait for God to make us his children and set our whole being free.

For it was by hope that we were saved; but if we see what we hope for, then it is not really hope. For who of us hopes for something we see? But if we hope for what we do not see, we wait for its with patience. But we hope for what we do not have then we wait for it patiently.

Roman 8:18-25

Faith is believed with conviction brings reality; Now that we had been put right with God through faith, we have peace with God through our Lord Jesus Christ. He has brought us by faith into this experience of God's grace, in which we now live. And so, we boast of the hope we have of sharing God's glory. **We also boast of our troubles, because we know that trouble produces endurance, endurance brings God's approval, and his approval creates hope. This hope does not disappoint us;** For God had poured out his love into our hearts by means of the Holy Spirit, who is God's gift to us. Roman 5:1-5

Anybody who had achieve great success in life did not achieve it from the memories of pleasure and happiness or extended ease and comfort but great success comes from diving into the sea of affliction and in the cellars of sufferings; Those who dive into the sea of affliction brings up rare pearls. Some Christian had paid the ultimate price for their faith and died from persecution and martyrdom. We must wear the thorn before we wear the crown. That is why the book of Revelation chapter 2 verses 26 says to everyone who overcomes, will be given power to rule all the nations.

That is why we never give up. For this reason, we never become discouraged. Even though our physical being is gradually decaying, yet our spiritual being is renewed day after day. And this temporary trouble we suffer will bring us a tremendous and eternal glory, much greater than the trouble. For we fix our eyes, not on the things that are seen, but on the things, that are not seen, what can be seen lasts only for a short time, but what cannot be seen lasts forever. 2 Corinthians 4; 16-18

Yesterday is history Tomorrow is a mystery today is a gift of God that is why we call it present

FACING CHALLENGES, YOU CAN OVERCOME; TURNING ADVERSITY/ANXIETY AND DEPPRESSION INTO OPPORTUINITY IS THE GREATEST BOOK EVER WRITTEN BY BISHOP ISAAC OGBETA; TO GIVE YOU HOPE AND STRENGTH AND COURAGE TO OVERCOME ALL CHALLENGES OF LIFE

FACING CHANLENGES, YOU CAN OVERCOME; IS THE GREATEST BOOK EVER WRITTEN BY BISHOP ISAAC OGBETA TO GIVE YOU HOPE AND COURAGE TO OVERCOME CHANLENGES OF LIFE AND TO GIVE YOU THE STRENGTH AND COURAGE TO TURN ADVERSITY/ANXIETY AND DEPRESSION INTO OPPORTUINITY

CHAPTER 2

Determination, Faith and Hope

Introduction; Some challenges facing you at this moment may include:

Challenges from an emotional trauma such as serious loss or death of a loved one : challenges of unemployment, challenges at work, challenges from school, challenges in personal relationship, such as marriage, divorce, Separation: lack of peace of mind:, Challenges from rejection or abandonment : challenges from financial stress: challenges from a serious medical illness: challenges from medication: challenges from a law-suit: challenges from imprisonment: challenges from jail term: challenges from Anxiety, Depression: challenges from addiction, such as cocaine, or heroin: challenges of rebellion from your children or love ones. Challenges from emotional or mental abuse: challenges from torment by demonic spirit; Challenges from loneliness or heartbrokenness. Challenges from fighting: Challenges of conflict or war: challenges as a refugee and homeless: challenges of suicide thought: Challenges of fear and the uncertainty of the future:

What you need most in order to overcome challenges are: Faith; Courage; resilience; persistence; and determination is what you needed most to overcome challenges:

First, you need FAITH:

Faith means to be sure of the things we hope for; to be certain of the things we cannot see. Believe with conviction brings reality.

It was by faith that the people of ancient times won God's approval. It was by faith that we understand that the universe was created by God's word, so what can be seen was made out of what cannot be seen. It was faith that made Abel offer to God a better sacrifice than Cain's. Through his faith he won God's approval as a righteous man, because God himself approved of his gifts. By means of his faith Abel still speaks, even though he is dead.

It was faith that kept Enoch from dying. Instead, he was taken up to God, and nobody could find him, because God had taken him up. The scriptures say that before Enoch was taken up, he had pleased God. No one can please God without faith, foe whoever comes to God must have faith that God exists and reward those who seek him.

It was faith that made Noah hear God's warning about things in the future that he could not see. He obeyed God and built a boat in which he and his family were saved. As a result, the world was condemned, and Noah received from God the righteousness that comes by faith. It was faith that made Abraham obeyed when God called him to go to a country which God had promised to give to him. He left his own country without knowing where he was going. By faith he lived as a foreigner in the country that God had promised him. He lived in tents, as did Isaac and Jacob, who received the same promise from God. For Abraham was waiting for the city which God had designed and built, the city with permanent foundations. It was faith that made Abraham able to become a father, even though he was too old and Sarah herself could not have children. He trusted God to keep his promise. Though Abraham was practically dead, from this one man came as many descendants as there are stars in the sky, as many as numberless grains of sand on the seashore. It was in faith that all these people died. They did not receive the things God had promised, but from a long way off they saw them and welcomed them and admitted that they were foreigners and refuges on earth. Those who say such things make it clear that they are looking for a country of their own. They did not keep thinking about the country they had left; if they had, they would have had the chance to return. Instead, it was a better country they longed for, the heavenly country. And so, God is not ashamed for them to call him their God, because he had prepared a city for them. It was faith that made Abraham offer his son Isaac as a sacrifice when God put Abraham to the test. Abraham was the one to whom God had made the promise, yet he was ready to offer his only son as a sacrifice. God had said to him, it is through Isaac that you would have the descendants that I promised. Abraham reckoned that God was able to raise Isaac from death. —and so, to speak, Abraham did receive Isaac back from death.

It was faith that made Isaac promise blessings for the future to Jacob and Esau. It was faith that made Jacob bless each of the sons of Joseph just before he died. He leaned on top of his walking sticks and worshipped God. It was faith that made Joseph, he was about to die, speak of the departure of the Israelites from Egypt, and leave instruction about what should be done with hid body. It was faith that made the parents of Moses hide him for three months after he was born. They saw that he was a beautiful child, and they were not afraid to disobey the kings order.

It was faith that made Moses, when he had grown up, refuse to be called the son of the king's daughter. He preferred to suffer with God's people rather than to enjoy sin for a little while. He reckoned that to suffer scorn for the Messiah was worth far more than all the reassures of Egypt, for he kept his eyes on the future reward. It was faith that made Moses leave Egypt without being afraid of the king's anger. As though he saw the invisible God, he refused to turn back. It was faith that made him establish the Passover and order the blood to be sprinkled on the doors, so that the angel of death would not kill the first-born sons of the Israelites. It was faith that made the Israelites able to cross the Red Sea as if on dry land; when the Egyptians tried to do it, the water swallowed them up. It was faith that made the walls of Jericho fall down after the Israelites marched around them seven days. It was faith that kept the prostitute Rahab from being killed with those who disobeyed God, for he gave the Israelites spies a friendly welcome. Should I go on? There is not enough time for me to speak of Gideon, Barak, Samson, Jephthah, David, Samuel, and the Prophets. Through faith they fought whole countries and won. They did what was right and received what God had promised. They shut the month of lions, put out fierce fires, escaped being killed by the swords. They were weak but became strong; they were mighty in battle and defeated the armies of foreigners. Through faith women received their dead relatives raised back to life. Others, refused to accept freedom, died under tortured in order to be raised to a better life. Some were mocked and whipped, others were put in chains and taken off to prison. They were stoned, they were sawed in two, they were killed by the sword. They went around clothed in skins of sheep or goats—poor persecuted, and mistreated. The world was not good enough for them. They wandered like refugees in the deserts and hills. Living in caves and in holes in the ground. What a record all of these have won by their faith; Yet they did not receive what God had promised, because God had decided on an even better plan for us. His purpose was that only in company with us would they be made perfect.

Secondly, you need Courage; Courage means the state or quality of mind or spirit that enables one to face danger, difficulty, pain, fear or vicissitudes without fear, with self-possession, confidence, and resolution; bravery, fearlessness, daring, valiant, valor, fortitude is the strength of mind that enables one to endure adversity. Bravery; nerve; fortitude; boldness; balls, pluck, grit, heroism; mettle; firmness, spunk, intrepidity. The states or condition of being a hero: Heroism. Bravery, Courageousness; Bold as a lion, bold as a martyr; Every challenge and every difficulty we successfully confront in life serves to strengthen our will, confidence and ability to conquer future obstacles, Herodotus, the Greek philosopher, said, "Adversity has the effect of drawing out strength and qualities of a man that would have lain dormant in its absence". When you respond positively and constructively to your biggest challenges, the qualities of strength, courage, character and perseverance emerge from deep inside of you. Of course, since we are human, it is very easy to get caught up in the self-pity, unfairness of life, or why me, or why did God allow this to happen to me? Trap, when we do, we fail to recognize the opportunities for wisdom and growth that accompany adversity. However, as soon as we allow ourselves to think more clearly, we are able to let go of self-defeating and unproductive thoughts and get down to the business of dealing with what's before us.

Thirdly you need Resilience to overcome adversity:

What is resilience? We all experience adversity, from everyday changes and challenges to serious losses. Fortunately, people are able to adapt. Resilience is the capacity to withstand stress and catastrophe. Psychologists have long recognized the capabilities of humans to adapt and to overcome risk and adversity. Individuals and communities are able to rebuild their lives even after devastating tragedies. Being resilience doesn't mean going through life without experiencing stress and pain. People feel grief, sadness, and a range of other emotions after adversity and loss. The road to resilience lies in working through the emotions and effects of stress and painful events. Resilience is also not something you are either born with or not. Resilience develops as people grow up and again better thinking and self-management skills and more knowledge. In most cases, it is called "The renewal of your mind". Resilience also comes from supportive relationships with parents, peers and others, as well as cultural beliefs and traditions that help people cope with inevitable bumps in life. Factors that contribute to resilience include: Close relationships with family and friends. A positive view of yourself and confidence in your strength and abilities: The ability to manage strong feelings and impulses: Good problem-solving and communication skills: Feeling in control: Seeking help and resources: Seeing yourself as resilient (rather than a victim): Coping with stress in healthy ways and avoiding harmful coping strategies, such as substance abuse: Helping others: Finding positive meaning in your life despite difficult or traumatic events.

CHAPTER 3

Turning Adversity into Opportunity/Advantage

This refers to the ability some people or companies have to take a bad situation and make it into a successful one; **Helen Keller was deaf and blind, meaning she lost her sight and hearing due to a mysterious fever.** She not only learned sign language, but earned a Bachelor of Arts degree, wrote 12 books and numerous articles, was a fundraiser for the blind, and campaigned for many liberal causes including women suffrage and workers' rights. She was awarded the Presidential Medal of Freedom and inducted into the national women's Hall of Fame. No one would have faulted her for living a quiet life of solitude, given her insurmountable disability. But she didn't. She was courageous and with determination overcame her blindness and her deafness.

Beethoven began to lose his hearing at the height of his career and eventually became completely deaf. So, he sawed the legs off his piano so he could set it on the floor and feel the vibrations as he played. His Symphony No. 9, of which he never had a single note, is one of the best-known works Classical music. He could have given in to the suicidal thoughts that over took him at first and become just another poetic tragedy. But he did not. **Elie Weisel and Viktor Frankl** experienced the unspeakable horrors of the Nazi concentration camps. Weisel went on to spread a massage of hope, atonement and peace, drawing from his own struggles to come to terms with the presence of evil in the world. He wrote over 40 books, including the acclaimed memoir Night, and he is a political activist for human justice, tolerance and freedom the world over. He was awarded the Noble Peace Prize for his crusades for human dignity. He could have become disillusioned, bitter and withdrawn from the world. Most of us probably would have after this kind of experience. But he didn't. From his own attempts to find a reason to keep living in the midst of meaningless suffering,

Frankl developed a philosophy that even in the cruelest and most hopeless of situations man has the ability to find internal meaning and purpose. He went on to teach that even when we are helpless to change the circumstances, we have within us to summon the will to live. He pioneered existential and humanist psychiatric systems and wrote more than 32 books, including his Hallmark Man's search for meaning. He could have broken and defeated by the horrors he experienced; Most of us could have given up but he did not.

Nelson Mandela spent 27 years as a political prisoner. He became a leader among his fellow inmates; fighting for better treatment, better food and study privileges, he earned his BA while imprisoned through a correspondence course by the University of London). He also became a symbol of hope and anti-apartheid resistance of his entire country. While behind bars, he continued to build his reputation as a political leader, refusing to compromise his beliefs to gain freedom, and upon his release, he led negotiations that resulted in the democracy he had always fought for. He was elected president of South Africa and received more than 250 Awards, including the Nobel Peace Prize. His funeral was a global event. He could have decided to lie low, to give in, and to let those 27 years sap his motivation and influence. But he didn't.

Albert Einstein, Alexander Graham Bell, Leonardo Da Vinci, Thomas Edison, Walt Disney and Winston Churchill are all said to have displaced signs of dyslexia and other learning disabilities. They did poorly in school. They were told they were stupid, talentless, unteachable, and that they would never amount to anything beyond "mediocre". I think you all knew they went on to do some impressive things. They could have believed in the negative voices and fail but they didn't. Speaking of Thomas Edison---In addition to failing about 10,000 times before landing on the successful design for the light bulb (I have not failed. I have just found 10,000 ways that won't work) His factory was burnt down to the ground when he was 67, destroying countless lab records of millions of dollars of equipment. When he surveys his losses, he remarked. There is great value in disaster. All our mistakes are burnt up thank God, we can start anew. He could have thrown in the towel at any of these set back, as seems "fate" was trying to tell him to but he didn't.

Winston Churchill; Overcame a stuttering problem and poor performance in school to become Prime Minister of United Kingdom and one the most influential political leaders of the twentieth century. He was also known for powerful and rousing speeches. **J K Rowling; She was born to a poor family and was a divorced single mother after a bad marriage, living on welfare, government assistance;** She wrote her first Harry Potter book and was turned down by most publishers until Bloomsbury Publishing picked it up. When she had the idea for the Harry Potter books she walked her baby in the stroller until it fell asleep, then she rushed to the nearest café to get out as many pages as she could before the baby woke up. She is now the revered master creator of a beloved global franchise and one of the richest women in the world. Determination, resilience, and persistence enabled all of these great people to push past their adversity and prevail, if they could do it, surely the rest of us can summon the strength and courage to do overcome our adversities. **Benjamin Franklin dropped out of school at the age of ten.** Franklin's parents could only afford to keep him in school until his tenth birthday. That didn't stop the great man from pursuing his education. He taught himself through voracious reading, and eventually went on to invent the lighting rod and bifocals. Oh, and he became one of America's Founding Fathers. **Stephen King's first novel was rejected 30 times.** If it weren't for King's wife, "Carrie" may not have ever existed. After being consistently rejected by publishing houses, King gave up and threw his first book in the trash. His wife, Tabitha, retrieved the manuscript and urged King to finish it. Now King's books have sold over 350 million copies and have been made into countless major motion pictures.

Jim Carrey used to be homeless. Carrey revealed to James Lipton on "Inside the Actor's Studio" that when he was 15, he had to drop out of school to support his family. His fathers were an unemployed musician and as the family went from "lower middle class to poor, "they eventually had to start living in a van. Carrey didn't let this stop him from his dream of becoming a comedian; He went from having his dad drive him to comedy clubs in Toronto to starring in mega-blockbusters and being known as one of the best comedic actors of an era. **Bill Gates' first business failed.** Yes, the richest person in the whole world couldn't make any money at first. Trad-O-Data: (a device which could read traffic tapes and process the date), was first Gate's company which failed miserably. When Gates and his partner, Paul Allen, tried to sell it, the product wouldn't even work. Gates and Allen didn't let that stop them from trying again though. This is how Allen explained how the failure helped them: Even though Traf-O-Data wasn't a roaring success, it was seminal in preparing us to make Microsoft's first product a couple of years later.'

CHAPTER **4**

What is Adversity and How to Overcome?

When circumstances or situation works against you, you face adversity; Adversity is a Latin word that comes from Adversitatem "opposition" and is related to the preposition, versus, a word common in legal or battle language meaning "against". What is the meaning of Adversity; A difficult period in your life which you have many problems,; we struggled in the face of adversity; A difficult or unlucky situation or event; A state of misfortune or affliction; a stroke of ill-fortune; a calamitous event; ILL- BEING (Lack of prosperity or happiness or health) CATASTROPHE, DISASTER (a state of extreme usually irremediable ruin and misfortune; EXTREMITY; an extreme condition or state or disease; VICTIMIZATION; adversity resulting from being made a victim; misfortune, ill luck, bad luck, trouble, difficulty, hardship, distress, disaster, suffering, affliction, sorrow, misery, tribulation, woe, pain, trauma ,calamity, bad break, catastrophe, clutch, downer,, evil eye, hard knocks, can of worms, hurting, mishap, pain in the neck, poison, kiss of death, jam, jinx, bummer, on the skids, contretemps, affliction. a state, condition, instance of serious or Continued difficulty or adverse fortune or fate; People show their through color in times of Adversity

Adversity is more than just one difficulty or set back. Adversity can be seen as series of difficulties or misfortune that keep you from achieving your goals and finding happiness. So how do you overcome it? You may think that all of the advice out there about overcoming adversity is easier said than done, but in reality, you too can overcome if you cultivate the right attitude and take steps to get what you want and deserve. If you want to start overcoming adversity today; then you must first need Faith, Hope, Love, Aid, Encouragement, Favor, Fortune, Help and Prosperity;

How to overcome adversity: By Faith you can overcome adversity; Faith from a Latin word means Fidem and from the Greek word means Pistis or Pisteuo; *Faith is the confidence that what you hope for is going to happen; A conviction that something you want is going to happen;* a determination to accomplish ones goal; complete trust or confidence in a person or thing or deity,; Trust, belief, confidence, conviction without a proof or evidence; For example you believe in the existence of God but you have not seen God before; Therefore you must have a confidence and conviction that God is able to bring you out from your adversity or crises or the situation you are going through; Strong or unshakable belief in something; having strong conviction without proof or evidence. Adjusting your perspective: means to change your approach or position on the way you interpret or approach things. This include the renewing of your mind. Secondly don't let your past dictate your future. Meaning if you fail ten times you can still make it. Thirdly; you must not quit or give up. Fourthly you must focus on the positive because focusing on the negative will bring you more depression. Fifth, accept the inevitability of adversity. Another thing you have to do is to accept the fact that adversity has to happen to everyone. Also, you need to build up your internal strength, and keep your composure as much as you can and take action. Find creative solution, have a rock-solid plan, be prepared to face the battle head on. Believe in yourself no matter what others have said about you, and you must take care of yourself and set your goals; Hebrew chapter 11 verses 1-40.

What is faith? Faith means to be sure of the things we hope for; to be certain of the things we cannot see; or It is the assurance that something we want is going to happen. It is the certainty that what we hope for is waiting for us, even though we cannot see it up ahead. Men of God in days of old were famous for their faith. By faith- by believing we know that the world and the stars - in fact, -all things-were made at God's command; and that they were all made from things that cannot be seen. It was by faith that Abel obeyed God and brought an offering that pleased God more than Cain's offering did. God accepted Abel and proved it by accepting his gift; and though Abel is long dead; we can still learn lessons from him about trusting God. Enoch trusted God too, and that is why God took him away to heaven without dying; suddenly he was gone because God took him. Before this happened, God had said how pleased he was with Enoch. You can never please God without faith, without depending on him. Anyone who wants to come to God must believe that there is a God and that he rewards those who sincerely look for him. Noah was another who trusted God. When he heard God's warning about the future, Noah believed in him even though there was then no sign of a flood, and wasting no time, he built the ark and saved his family. Noah's belief in God was in direct contrast to the sin and disbelief of the rest of the world— which refused to obey—and because of his faith he became one of those whom God has accepted.

Abraham trusted God, and when God told him to leave home and go far away to another land that he promised to give to him, Abraham obeyed. Away he went, not even knowing where he was going. And even when he reached God's Promised Land, he lived in tents like a mere visitor as did Isaac and Jacob, to whom God gave the promise. Abraham did this because he was confidently waiting for God to bring him to that strong heavenly city whose designer and builder is God. Sarah, too, had faith, and because of this she was able to become a mother in spite of her old age, for she realized that God, who gave her his promise, would certainly do what he said. And so, a whole nation came from Abraham, who was too old to have even one child—a nation with so many millions of people that, like the stars of the sky and the sand on the sea shores, there is no way to count them. These men of faith I have mentioned died ever receiving all that God had promised them; but they saw it all awaiting them on ahead and were glad, for they agreed that this earth was not their real home but that they were just strangers visiting down here. And quiet obviously when they talked like that, they were looking forward to their real home in heaven. If they had wanted to, they could have gone back to the good things of this world. But they didn't want to. They were living for heaven. And now God is not ashamed to be called their God, for he has made a heavenly city for them.

While God was testing him, Abraham still trusted in God and his promises, and so he offered up his son Isaac, and was ready to slay him on the altar of sacrifice; yes, to slay even Isaac, through whom God had promised to give Abraham, many descendants. He believed that if Isaac died God would bring him back to life again; and that is just about what happened, for as far as Abraham was concerned, Isaac was doomed to death, but he came back again alive. It was by faith that Isaac knew God would give future blessings to his two sons, Jacob and Esau. By faith Jacob, when he was old and dying, blessed each of Joseph's two sons as he stood and prayed, leaning on the top of his cane. And it was by faith that Joseph, as he neared the end of his life, confidently spoke of God bringing the people of Israel out of Egypt; and he was so sure of it that he made them promise to carry his bones with them when they left. Moses parents had faith too, when they saw that God had given them an unusual child, they trusted that God would save him from the death the king commanded, and they hid him for three months and were not afraid. It was by faith that Moses, when he grew up, refused to be treated as the grandson of the king, but chose to share ill-treatment with God's people instead of enjoying fleeting pleasures of sin. He thought that it was better to suffer for the promised Christ than to own all the treasures of Egypt, for he was looking forward to the great reward that God would give him. And it was because he trusted God that he left the land of Egypt and wasn't afraid of the king's anger;

Moses kept right on going: it seemed as though he could see God right there with him. And it was because he believed God would save his people that he commanded them to kill a lamb as God had told them to sprinkle the blood on the doorposts of their homes so that God's terrible Angel of Death could not touch the oldest child in those homes as he did among the Egyptians. The people of Israel trusted God and went right through the Red Sea as though they were on dry ground. But when the Egyptians chasing them tried it, they were drowned. It was by faith that brought the walls of Jericho tumbling down after the people of Israel had walked around them seven days as God has commanded them. By faith –because she believed in God and his power—Rehab the harlot did not die with all the others in her city when they refused to obey God, for she gave a friendly welcome to the spies.

THE GLORIOUS MESSIAH AND THE MESSIANIC AGE

BOOK OF ISHIAH CHAPTER 9 : 1 ; For this section of the notes I shall provide a fully written exposition of the text to demonstrate how the exegetical details can be incorporated into an expository style. The length of the time allowed for the exposition will determined in the exegetical process what the central theological ideas are; I will be able to condense around them rather easily. In spite of all the advances of civilization, the world today is still consumed with a desire for peace and a fear of war. When people observe the conflicts and the rumors of wars, gloom and despair often engulf them like thick darkness. Not the least of the trouble spots in the Middle East.

Peace there has been the pursuit for centuries. While there have been scores of efforts to bring about peace between Israel and Syria and the Palestinians, no one would be surprised if

war broke out tomorrow. Peace movements and peace negotiations proceed all over the world. Stronger countries believe
that peace must be negotiated from a position of power; radi-
cal groups believe that terror will force the issue. But we are
left with a more dangerous and more frightening world than
ever before. And we are left wondering if anyone is really in-
terested in peace and righteousness and justice for all, or just
securing their own interests? The problem is still the presence
of evil in this world. It set brother against brother, and nations
against nation.

Ultimately, the world's gloom and despair is linked to spiritual
darkness. The bible comforts and reminds those of us who
have come to trust in Jesus Christ not to despair as if there was
no hope. WE have the revelation of our Lord that not only
announces His Sovereign reign but also charts the course of
world events. One of the most significant revelations is found
in the book of Isaiah chapter 9. Against the background of the
prophecy of war and destruction, darkness and gloom (chapter
8) Isaiah gave this prophecy about the Messiah---the glorious
coming king. "Messiah" is a Hebrew term that means "anointed one," that is, the anointed king. In a sense, every king who
was anointed in Jerusalem as a descendant of David would be
called a "messiah." (Pronounced Ham-she-ack), a Messiah:
But the bible tells how ultimately a son of David would come
who would be known as "the Messiah. "We believe that Jesus
Christ is that Messiah. The New Testament word "Christ" is
the Greek translation of the Hebrew word "Messiah." This
Messianic Prophecy, then, holds out hope for peace and righteousness through the reign of Jesus the Messiah. The text can
be divided into two sections: The Dawn of the Messianic Age
(verses 1-5 and the Righteous Reign of the Messiah (verses 6

and 7). While the entire passage is instructive for the message, the verses that focus on the nature of the Messiah are critical, for therein lies our hope for everlasting peace. So, most of our attention will be given to the meanings of the Son, showing how this description fit perfectly the nature of our Lord Jesus Christ. **Exposition; Peace will come with the dawn of the Messianic age: Isaiah Chapter 9 verses 1-5):** Isaiah declares that in contrast to his present age of war, gloom, and despair, there is coming an age when peace will reign universally. It will begin with the coming of the Messiah, the promised future king. So, we call that period the Messianic Age. The prophet here shows how it will unfold.

The change in circumstances will end the despair. The passage begins with the announcement of the change: There will be no more gloom for those in anguish; in the past, the Lord humbled the northern lands of Zebulun and Naphtali, but in the future, he will honor Galilee. Why? That is where the Messiah will first appear—Galilees of the Gentiles, a place looked down on for so long as less spiritual, less pure than Judea. The explanation of this exaltation is found in verses 2. Those who walk in darkness have seen a great light, on those in the shadow of death a light has dawned. The language is poetic; darkness signifies adversity, despair, gloom and evil, and the light signifies prosperity, peace, and joy. The language is used elsewhere of the Messianic age—the book of Malachi says that the "sun of righteousness will rise with healing in his wings" (4:2). So, the people in the north who have suffered so much have the prospect of a wonderful new beginning. We should note in passing that Isaiah's verbs are in the past tense—he writes as if it has already happened. That is prophetic language. The prophet was a "seer" or visionary. He received a divine revelation and recorded what he saw. As far as he was concerned, if it had been shown to him from God, it was as good as done. It was certain even though it had not yet worked out in the history. So "light" will shine on people who were walking in "darkness." The initial fulfillment of this prophecy is beyond doubt. Matthew quotes this text in conjunction with the beginning of Jesus Ministry in Galilee. He is the true light of the world that lights every person. He brings to a darkened world grace and truth, and the sure promised of truth, and the sure promised of peace. When He began to minster in Galilee with His teachings and His miracles, He demonstrated that indeed He was this Messiah. His proclamation of the kingdom through salvation is what ends the despair, for believers in Him are not lost in gloom and despair, for they know that what He promised will come to pass at His second coming.

The Messiah brings joy and prosperity: The prophet turns to address the Lord directly. His words explain what it means that light will dispel the darkness—joy and prosperity will follow. The prophet gives no clue as to how soon this will happen. But we who have a full revelation of God know that Jesus made it clear that He was the Messiah and that the age of peace and Righteousness was yet future. The joy described here is extravagant. It is the kind of joy that comes at the harvest, or at the dividing of the plunder. Harvest was a regular time of joy in Israel; after a long time of labor in the fields the people would gather to eat and drink and celebrate. The bible often uses the analogy of the harvest to describe the coming of the Lord. (Read the book of Matthew 3:12 for the harvest and winnowing imagery). It is the thanksgiving celebration for the completion of the harvest. Dividing the plunder, the other image here, is a bit more poignant since wars will lead up to the end of age. The image is about the victors after the battle is over, dividing up the booty. Such would be an almost delirious celebration of triumph that would usher in an age of peace.

Joy comes through the cessation of war: The imagery of joy at the division of the plunder leads directly into the explanation: the prophet foresees the time when the Lord will break the oppression of the enemies. He draws the analogy with the time of Israel's victory over the Medians through Gideon by the power of the Lord. So shall it again be. But this victory will be greater. Verses 5 say that the implementation of war will be burnt up. This will be no lull in the action, no temporary treaty. War will end. Elsewhere Isaiah has said "They shall beat their swords into ploughshares," that is, military weapon will not be needed in a time of lasting peace. How can these things be, given the world situation as we know it? The answer to this question is found in the second half of the oracle which describes the nature of the Messiah who will bring in the reign of peace and righteousness. If such peace is to come, someone must have the ability to produce and maintain it. **Peace will finally come with righteous reign of the Messiah:** (The book of Isaiah chapter 9 verses 6-7). Isaiah now turns to introduce the One who will transform the gloom and despair of war into joy and peace of a time of righteousness—the Messiah. The Lord will bring the advent of the Messiah. The first part of the prophecy is very familiar to Christians:

For to us a child is born, and unto us a son is given, and the government shall be upon his shoulder, and he shall reign for ever and ever. Isaiah is very precise here, as we know. A child will be born into the family of David, and that there was a birth in Bethlehem is beyond question; but the Messiah will also be the son that is given, and that Jesus did not come into existence in Bethlehem is clear from the bible. According to the Davidic Covenant (the book of 2 Samuel chapters 7 verse 14), the term "Son" is a title for the king. The same is true in the vision of Daniel where the expression "Son of Man" is used (7:9-14). Daniel's vision shows this glorious king in the presence of the Almighty, the Ancient of Days, and that he would be given the kingdom of peace. Isaiah announces that the child to be born will be this Son given. This idea then clarified by Paul: "In the fullness of time, God sent forth His Son, born of a woman" --- (The book of Galatians chapter 4 verses 4). The New Testament bears witness that Jesus is this Son who came into the world. In fact, Jesus Himself set about to prove His origin was in heaven, not in Bethlehem. When He was about to raise Lazarus from the dead, he prayed and included these words in His prayers: "that they might know that you sent Me" (John 11:42). By this he meant that He was from above, and they were from below. Or, in debating with the religions leaders Jesus asked how David could call his descendant his "Lord, "clearly showing that the "Son of David," the Messiah, was greater than David (the book of Mark chapter 12 verses 35-36 and Psalms 110). And of course, to the woman at the well Jesus clearly revealed himself: she said, "When the Messiah comes, He will declare all things to us. "Jesus said, "I that speak to you am He" (John 4:25-26). It is clearly, then, that Jesus claimed to be the Messiah, the Christ, the child born into the house of David, the Son given by God to be the long-expected king. The first advent of Jesus established His identity; it not begins his reign, however, for He has yet to put down all enemies. The prophecy that "the government will be upon His shoulder" will come to complete reality at His second coming—an aspect of the Messianic prophecies that the prophet did not see (1 Peter 1:10-11). The reference to the shoulder is probably a reference to the wearing of an insignia of office on the shoulder (The book of Isaiah chapter 22:22) There will be a time when this Son will rule as king. We may say that Jesus now reigns above, and that is certainly true. But Isaiah envisions a time of universal peace and righteousness in this world. That has not happened yet. Hebrew 1 states that this exaltation will be complete when the Father again brings His firstborn into the world. So Isaiah does not know when all these things will take place; only they will happen because the word of the Lord has declared it. **The Messiah will be a wonder king:** The nature of the Messiah is now portrayed in the listing of His Throne names. It must be noted that these are not names in the sense that we have names. These are character descriptions. They intended to give the nature or significance of the person named. We use the word "name" at times in this way. We may say, "She made a name for herself, "that is, a reputation. **The names in this section describe the nature of the glorious king.** (46)

When Job lost everything, God was not done yet: The book of Job Chapter 42: the book of Job. The Midrash says that Moses would console with it the Israelites while they were suffering in Egypt". The Midrashim source referred to here has never been pointed. Furthermore, according to Malbim, Job never doubted God or shifted from a position of absolute faith in moral righteousness of God's actions in the world. Job is consoling and heartening because there is a lesson that if one trusts in the Lord and follows His ways, all will be well in the end. As we find: But they who trust in the Lord shall renew their strength, as eagles grow new plumes. They shall run and grow not weary. They shall march and not grow faint. Isaiah 40:31. THE HAPPY ENDING; In his commentary to Job 42:10-12, Malbim maintains that God returned to Job all his children and increased his property to twice what it was before. Here Malbim refers to unnamed Midrashim that states that Satan merely captured and held his children and his property and then released them unharmed --restoring all to Job. As an apparent to the sagas, Job's properties were not despoiled and his children did not die. Only Satan hid them from his face and sent him a massager to bring him evil tidings. All his property and his children were the whole time in the hands of Satan.

Adversity is the prosperity of the great:

By Hope; and through hoping you can turn adversity into opportunity/advantage. Hope is a feeling expectation and desire for certain things to happen, aspiration, desire; wish; expectation; ambition; aim; goal , plan ,design; to wish for something with expectation of its fulfillment; to have confidence or trust. A wish or desire accompanied by confident expectation of its fulfillment. You want something to happen, expect, anticipation. Despair looks at immediate realities. Hope sees final and ultimate realities. Hope can be sustained by trusting God. Hopelessness is a curse; it is the curse of trusting in a man or your own self or in anything other than God in his perfect wisdom and timing.

Hope is the feeling we have that, the feeling we have is not the feeling we will have. Someone sees a hopeless end; others see endless hope. Psalms 33 verses 17 say the war horse is a false hope for salvation. *Hope is the (up) feeling we have that the (down) feeling is not permanent. Roman chapter 15 verses 12-13 says and the prophet Isaiah said "There shall be an Heir in the house of Jesse, and he will be the king over the Gentiles; they will pin their hope on him alone." So, I pray for you Gentiles that God who gives you hope will keep you happy and full of peace as you believe in him. Roman chapter 5 verses 2-5 says "For because of our faith, he has brought us into this place of highest privilege where we now stand, and we confidently and joyfully look forward to actually becoming all that God has had in mind for us to be.* **We can now rejoice too, when we run into problems and trials (Adversity): For we know that they are good for us—they help us learn to be patience. And Patience develops strength of character in us and helps us trust God more each time we use it until finally our hope and faith are strong and steady. Then, when that happens and know that all is well, for we know how dearly God loves us, and we feel this warm love everywhere within us the Holy Spirit to feel our heart with love. (Roman Chapter 5 verses 2-5)**

God is not done yet, no matter what you are going through in your life right now; Because God was not done yet---When Job lost everything

- When Sarah was barren
- When Joseph was in prison
- When Moses was on the run from Pharaoh
- When the children of Israel were pinned against Red Sea

- When, walls of Jericho blocked, the possession, of the Promised Land
- When Gideon was hiding from the Mediante When
- Samson was seduced by a woman and blinded;
- When Ruth was windowed
- When David was mocked as a boy facing the giant
- When Jonah was in the belly of the fish
- When Job lost everything
- Paul could not get rid of his torn.
- When Noah was in the boat

CHAPTER 5

David Faced Goliath

David was mocked as boy when facing Goliath: 1 Samuel chapter 16, 17, The Lord said to Samuel, "How long will you grieve over Saul? I have rejected him from being king over Israel. Fill your horn with oil and set out; I will send you to Jesse the Bethlehemite, for I have provided for myself a king among his sons. Samuel said, "How can I go? If Saul hears of it he will kill me. And the Lord said takes a heifer with you, and say, I have come to sacrifice to the Lord. Invite Jesse to the sacrifice, and I will show you what you shall do; and you shall anoint for me one whom I named to you. Samuel did what the Lord commanded and came to Bethlehem. The elders of the city came to meet him trembling, and said, "Do you come peacefully? He said peacefully I have come to sacrifice to the Lord: Sanctify yourself and come with me to the sacrifice. And he sanctifies Jesse and his sons and invited them to the sacrifice. When they came he looked on Eliab and thought, "Surely the Lord's anointed is now before the Lord." But the Lord said to Samuel do not look on his appearance or on the height of his stature, because I have rejected him; for the Lord does not see as mortals see; "they looked on the

outward appearance, but the Lord looks on the heart." Then
Jesse called on Abinadab and made him pass before Samuel.
He said, "Neither has the Lord chosen this one. Then Jesse
made Shammah pass by. And he said, "Neither has the Lord
chosen this one. Jesse made his seven of his sons pass before
Samuel, and Samuel said to Jesse the Lord has not chosen any
of these." Samuel said to Jesse are all your sons here? And
he said there remains yet the youngest, but he is keeping the
sheep." And Samuel said to Jesse, "send and bring him; for we
will not sit down until he comes here. He sent and brought
him in. Now he was ruddy, and had beautiful eyes, and was
handsome. The Lord said, "Rise and anoint him; for this is the
one." Then Samuel took the oil and anointed him in the presence of his brothers; and the Spirit of the Lord came mightily
upon David from that day forward. Samuel set out and went
to Ramah. Now the Spirit of the Lord departed from Saul, and
an evil Spirit from the Lord tormented him. And Saul servant
said to him, "See now, an evil spirit from God is tormenting
you." Let our lord now command the servants who attend
you to look for someone who is skillful in playing the Lyre;
and when the evil spirit from the Lord, is upon you, he will
play it, and you will feel better. So, Saul said to his servants,
"Provide me someone who can play well, and bring him to
me." One of the young men answered," I have seen a son of
Jesse the Bethlehemite who is skillful in playing, a man of
valor, a worrier, prudent in speech; and the Lord is with him."
So, Saul sent massagers to Jesse, and said, "Send me your son
David who is with the sheep." Jesse took a donkey loaded
with bread, a skin of wine, and a kid, and sent them by his son
David to Saul. And David came to Saul, and entered his ser-
vice. Saul loved him greatly, and he became his armor-bearer.
Saul sent to Jesse, saying; let David remain in my service, for

he has found favor in my sight." And whenever the evil spirit from God came upon Saul, David took the lyre and played it in his hand, and Saul will be relieved, and feel better, and the evil spirit would depart from him.

The battlefield: David challenged Goliath: 1 Samuel chapter 17; Now the Philistines gathered their armies for battle; they were gathered at Socoh, which belongs to Judah, and encamped between Socoh and Azekah, in Ephes-dammim. Saul and the Israelites gathered and emcamped in the valley of Elah, and formed ranks against the Philistines. The Philistine stood on the mountain on the one side, and Israel stood on the mountain on the other sides, with a valley between them. And there came out from the camp of the Philistines a champion named, Goliath, of Gath, whose height was six cubits and a span. He had helmets of bronze in his head, and he was armed with a coat of mail; the weight of the coat was five thousand shekels of bronze. He has greaves of bronze on his legs and a javelin of bronze slung between his shoulders. The shaft of his spear was like a weaver's beam, and his spear's head weighs six hundred shekels of iron; and his shield-bearer went before him. He stood and shouted to the ranks of Israel, "Why have you come out to draw out for battle? Am I not a Philistine, and are you not servants of Saul? Choose a man for yourselves and let him come down to me. If he is able to fight with me and kill me, then we will be your servants; but if I prevail against him and kill him, then you shall be our servants and serve us; And the Philistine said, "Today I defy the ranks of Israel. Give me a man that we may fight together." When Saul and all the Israelites heard these words of the Philistine, they were dismayed and greatly afraid. Now David was the son of an Ephrathite of Bethlehem in Judah who had eight sons. In the days of Saul Jesse was old and well on in years. The three oldest sons of Jesse had followed Saul to war; the names of these three sons who had gone off to war were Eliab the first born; Abinanba the second; and Shammah the third. David was the youngest. While the three oldest had join Saul, David would come and go from Saul's presence to tend his father's sheep at Bethlehem. Meanwhile the Philistine came forward and took his stand morning and evening for forty days. Now Jesse said to his son David: "Take this ephah of roasted grain and these ten loaves for your brothers, and bring them quickly to your brothers in the camp. Also take these ten cheeses for the field officer. Greet your brothers and bring home some token from them. Saul and your brothers, together with all Israel, are at war with the Philistines in the valley of the Elah. Early the next morning, having left the flock with a shepherd, David pack up and set out, as Jesse had commanded him. He reached the barricade of the camp just as the armies, on their way to the battleground, were shouting their battle cry. The Israelites and the Philistines drew up opposite each other in battle array. David entrusted what he had brought to the keeper of the baggage and hastened to the battle line, where he greeted his brothers. While he was talking with them, the Philistine champion, by named Goliath of Gath, came up from the ranks of the Philistines, and spoke as before, and David listened. When the Israelites saw the man, they all retreated before him terrified. The Israelites had been saying; do you see this man coming up? He comes up to insult Israel. The king will make whoever kills him a very wealthy man. He will give his daughters to him and declares his father's family except from the taxes in Israel. David now said to the men standing near him, "How will the man who kills this Philistine and freed Israel from disgrace be reward?

Who is this uncircumcised Philistine that he should insult the armies of the living God? They repeated the same word to him and said, that is how the man who kills him will be rewarded. When Eliab, the oldest brother, heard him speaking with the men, he grew angry with David and said: Why do you come down? With whom have you left those sheep in the wilderness? I know your arrogance and your dishonest heart. You came down to enjoy the battle. David protested, what have I done now? I was only talking.

He turned from him to another and asked the same question; and everyone gave him the same answer as before. The words that David had spoken were overheard and reported to Saul, who sent for him. David Challenge Goliath: Then David spoke to Saul: "My Lord should not loose heart. Let your servants go and fight this Philistine." But Saul answered David, "You cannot go up against this Philistine and fight with him, for you are only a youth, while he has been a warrior from his youth." Then David told Saul: "Your servants used to tend his father's sheep and whenever a lion or bear came to carry off a sheep from the flock, I would chase after it, attack it, and snatch the prey from its month. If it attacked me, I would seize it by the throat, strike it, and then kill it. Your servants had killed both a lion and a bear. This uncircumcised Philistine will be as one of them, because he has insulted the armies of the living God. David continued: "The same God who delivers me from the claws of lion and the bear will deliver me from the hands of this Philistine. Saul answered David; "Go the Lord will be with you."

Preparation for the encounter: Then Saul dressed David in his own tunic, putting a bronze helmet on his head and arming him with a coat of mail. David also fastened the sword of Saul over the tunic. He walked with difficulty, however, since he had not worn armor before. He said to Saul, "I cannot go in these, because I am not used to them. So, he took them off. Then, staff in hand, David selected five smooth's stone from the way and put them in the pocket of his shepherd's bag. With his sling in hand, he approached the Philistine.

David Victory: with his shield-bearer marching before him, the Philistine advanced closer and closer to David. When he sized David up and saw that he was youthful, ruddy, and handsome in appearance, he began to deride him. He said to David, "Am I a dog that you come against me with a staff? "Then the Philistine cursed David by his gods and he said to him, "Come here to me, and I will feed your flesh to the birds of the air and the beast of the field. "David answered him: "You come against me with sword and spear and scimitar, but I come against you in the Name of the Lord of hosts, the God of the armies of Israel whom you have insulted. Today the Lord shall deliver you into my hand; I will strike you down and cut off head. This very day I will feed your dead body and the dead bodies of the Philistine army to the birds of the air and to the beast of the field; thus, the whole land shall have learnt that Israel has a God, and all this multitude, too, shall learn that it is not by sword or spear that the Lord saves. **For the battle belongs to the Lord, who shall deliver you into our hands:** Then the Philistine then moved to meet David at close quarters, while David ran quickly towards the battle line to meet the Philistine. David put his hand into the bag and put out a stone, hurled it with the sling, and he struck Philistine on the forehead. The stone embedded itself in his brow, and he fell on his face to the ground. Thus, David triumphed over the Philistine with sling and stone; he stuck the Philistine dead, and did it without a sword in his hand. Then David ran and stood over him; with the Philistines, own sword which he drew from his sheath he killed him, and cut off his head In Jesus name. When the Philistines saw that their hero was dead, they fled. Then the men of Israel and Judah sprang up with a battle cry and pursued them to the approaches of Gath and to the gates of Ekron, and Philistines fell along wounded along the road from shaaraim as far as Gath and Ekron. When they have returned from the pursuit of the Philistines, the Israelites looted their camp. David took the head of the Philistine and brought it to Jerusalem; but he kept Goliath's armor in his own tent.

CHAPTER 6

Jesus Death and Resurrection

When Moses was running for his life from King Pharaoh of Egypt

Moses flight to Midian: On one occasion, after Moses had grown up, when he visited his kinsmen and witness their forced labor, he saw an Egyptian striking a Hebrew, one of his own kinsmen. Looking about and seeing no one, he slew the Egyptian and hid him in the sand. The next day he went out again, and now two Hebrew were fighting: So, he asked the culprit, "why are you striking your fellow Hebrew?" But he replied, "Who has appointed you a ruler and a judge over us? Are thinking of killing me as you killed the Egyptian? Then Moses became afraid and thought, "The affair must certainly be known." Pharaoh, too, also heard of the affair and sought to put him to death. But Moses fled from him and stayed in the Land of Midian.

As he seated there by a well, seven daughters of a priest of Midian came to draw water and fill the troughs to water their father's flocks. But some shepherds came and drove them away. Then Moses got up and defended them, and watered their flocks. When they returned to their father Reuel, he said to them, "How is it that you have returned so soon today?" "They answered, "An Egyptian saved us from interference of the shepherds. He even drew water for us and watered the flock. "Where is the man?" he asked his daughters. "Why did you leave him there? Invite him to have something to eat." Moses agreed to live with him, and the man gave him his daughter Zipporah in marriage. She bore him a son, whom he named Gershom; for he said," I am a stranger in a foreign land.

The burning bush: A long time passed, during which the king of Egypt died. Still the Israelites groaned and cried out because of their slavery. As their cry for release went up to God, he heard their groaning and was mindful of his covenant with Abraham, Isaac and Jacob. He saw the Israelites and knew--- "Meanwhile Moses was tending the flock of his father in law Jethro, the priest of Midian." Leading the flock across the desert, he came to Horeb, the mountain of God. There an angel of the Lord appeared to him in fire flaming out of the bush. As he looked on, he was surprised to see that the bush, though on fire, was not consumed. So, Moses decided, "I must go over to look this remarkable sight, and see why the bush is not burned."

The call of Moses: When the Lord saw him, coming over to look at it more closely, God called out to him from the bush, "Moses, Moses," he answered, "Here I am." God said, come no nearer, Remove the sandals from your feet, for the place where you stand is holy ground am the God of your father, he continued, "The God of Abraham, the God of Isaac, the God of Jacob. Moses hid his face, for he was afraid to look at God. But the Lord said, "I have witnessed the affliction of my people who are in Egypt and have heard their cry of complaint against their slave drivers, so I know well what they are suffering. Therefore, I have come down to rescue them from the hands of the Egyptians and lead them out of that land into a good and spacious land, a land flowing with milk and honey, the country of the Canaanites and Jebusites. Indeed, the cry of the Israelites has reached me, and I have truly noted that the Egyptians are oppressing them. Come, now. I will send you to Pharaoh to lead my people, the Israelites, out of Egypt. But Moses said to God who am I that I should go to Pharaoh and lead the Israelites out of Egypt? He answered, **I will be with you:**

When Jesus was put into the grave: Luke: 23:26. The Soldiers led Jesus away, and as they were going, they met a man from Cyrene named Simon who was coming into the city from the country. They seized him, put the cross on him, and made him carry it before Jesus. A large crowd of people followed him; among them were some women who were weeping and wailing for him. Jesus turned to them and said,

Women of Jerusalem; don't cry for me, but yourself and for your children: For the days are coming when people will say, how lucky are the women who never had children, who never bore babies, who never nursed them. That will be the time when people will say to the mountains, fall on us, and to the hills, hide us.

For if such things are done when the wood is green, what will happen when it is dry?

Luke: 26-31. Two other men, both of them criminals, were also led out to be put to death with Jesus. When they came to the place called "The Skull," they crucified Jesus there, and the two criminals, one on his right, then the other on his left. Jesus said "Forgive them Father; they don't know what they are doing." They divided his clothes among themselves by throwing dice. The people stood there watching while the Jewish leaders made fun of him: "He saved others, let him save himself if he is the Messiah whom God has chosen." The soldiers also made fun of him: they came up to him and offered him cheap wine, and said save yourself if you are the king of the Jews. Above him were written these words: "**This is the King of the Jews:** One of the criminals hanging there hurled insults at him, "Aren't you the Messiah? Save yourself and us. The other one however rebuked him, saying, don't you fear God? You received the same sentence he did. Ours, however, is only right, because we are getting what we deserve for what we did: but he has done no wrong. And he said to Jesus, "Remember me, Jesus, when you come as a king. Jesus said to him, "I promise you that today you will be in Paradise with me: It was about twelve o'clock when the sun stopped shinning and darkness covered the whole country until three o'clock; and the curtain hanging in the temple was torn in two. Jesus cried out in a loud voice, "Father in your hands I placed my Spirit. "He said this and died. The army officer what had happened and he praised God, saying, certainly he was the son of God. When the people we had gathered there to watch the spectacle saw what had happened, they all went back home, beating their breasts in sorrow. All those who knew Jesus personally, including the women who had followed him from Galilee, stood at distance to watch. There was a man named Joseph from Arimathea, a town in Judea.

He was a good and honorable man, who was waiting for the coming of the Kingdom of God. Although he was a member of the council, he had not agreed with their decision and action. He went into the presence of Pilate and asked for the body of Jesus. Then he took the body down, wrapped it in a linen sheet, and placed it in a tomb which had been dug out solid rock and which had never been used. It was Friday, and the Sabbath was about to begin. The women who had followed Jesus from Galilee went with Joseph and saw the tomb and how Jesus body was placed on it. Then they went back home and prepared the spies and perfumes for the body. On the Sabbath, they rested as the Law commanded.

JESUS ROSE FROM THE DEAD; HE IS RISEN; Very early on Sunday morning the women went to the tomb, carrying the spies they had prepared. They found the stone rolled away from the entrance to the tomb, so they went in; but they did not find the body of the Lord Jesus. They stood there puzzled about this, when suddenly two men in bright shining clothes stood by them. Full of fear, the women bowed down to the ground, as the men said to them, "Why are you looking among the dead for one who is alive? He is not here; he has been raised. Remember what he said to you while he was in Galilee; The Son of Man must be handed over to sinners, be crucified, and three days later rise to life. Then the women remembered his words, returned from the tomb, and told all these things to the eleven disciples and all the rest.

The women were Mary Magdalene, Joanna, and Mary the mother of James; they and the other women with them told these things to the apostles. But the apostles thought that what the women said was nonsense, and they did not believe them. But Peter got up and ran to the tomb; he bent down and saw the clothes but nothing else; Then he went back home amazed at what had happened; **The walk to Emmaus:** On that same day two of Jesus followers were going to a village called Emmaus, about seven miles from Jerusalem, and they were talking to each other about all the things that had happened. As they talked and discussed, Jesus himself drew near and walked along with them; they saw him, but somehow did not recognize him. Jesus said to them, "What are you talking about to each other, as you walk along?" They stood still, with sad faces. One of them, named Cleopas, asked him, "Are you the only visitor in Jerusalem who doesn't know the things that have been happening there these last few days? "What things?" he asked. "The things that happened to Jesus of Nazareth," they answered. "This man was a prophet and was considered by God and by all the people to be powerful in everything he said and did. Our chief Priests and rulers handed him over to be sentenced to death, and he was crucified. And we had hoped that he would be the one who was going to set Israel free. Besides all that, this is the third day since it happened. Some of the women of our group surprised us; they went at dawn to the tomb, but could not find his body. They came back saying they had seen a vision of angels who told them that he is alive. Some of our group went to the tomb and found it exactly as the women has said, but they did not see him. Then Jesus said to them, how foolish you are how slow you are to believe everything the prophets said; was it not necessary for the Messiah to suffer these things and then to enter his glory?" And Jesus explained to them what was said about himself in all Scriptures, beginning with the books of Moses and writings of all the prophets. As they came near the village to which they were going, Jesus acted as if he were going further; but they held him back, saying, stay with us; the day is almost over and it is getting dark. So he went in to stay with them. He sat down to eat with them, took the bread, and said the blessings; then he broke the bread and gave it to them. Then their eyes were opened and they recognized him, but he disappeared from their sights. They said to each other, "Wasn't it like fire burning in us when he talked to us on the road and explained the Scriptures to us? They got up at once and went back to Jerusalem, where they found the eleven disciples gathered together with the others, and saying, The Lord is raised indeed. He had appeared to Simon. The two then explained to them what had happened on the road, and how they had recognized the Lord when he broke the bread.

Never give up hope: John chapter 15 verses 18 says, "If the world hates you, realize that it hated me first. If you belonged to the world, the world would love his type of people: but because you do not belong to the world, and I have chosen you out of the world, the world hates you. Remember the word I spoke to you; no slave is greater than his master. If they persecuted me, they will also persecute you. If they kept my word they will also keep yours. And they will do all these things to you on account of my name because they do not know the one who sent me. If I have not come and spoken to them, they would have no sin; but as it is they have no excuse for their sin. Whoever hates me, also hates my father. If I have not done a works among them that no one else ever did, they would have no sin; but as it's, they have seen and hated both me and my father. But in order that the word written in their law might be fulfilled, they hated me without a cause. When the Advocate comes whom I will send you from the father, he will testify to me. And you also testify to me, because you have been with me from the beginning. Chapter 16:1. I have told you this so that you may not fall away. They will expel you from the synagogues; in fact, the hour is coming when everyone who kills you will think he is offering worship to God. They will do this because they have not known the father or me. I have told you this so that when the hour comes you may remember that I told you.

Jesus departure and the coming of the advocate: I did not tell you this from the beginning, because I was with you. But now I am going to the one who sent me, and not one of you asks me, where are you going? But because I told you this, grief has filled your hearts. But I tell you the truth, it is better for you that I go. For if I do not go, the Advocate will not come to you. But if I go, I will send you the Advocate. And when he comes he will convict the world in regard to sin and righteousness, and condemnation: Sin, because they did not believe in me; righteousness because I am going to the father and you will no longer sees me; Condemnation: because the ruler of this world has been condemned. I have much more to tell you, but you cannot bear it now. But when he comes, the Spirit of truth will guide you to all truth. He will not speak of his own, but he will speak what he hears, and will declare to you the things that are coming. He will glorify me, because he will take from what is mine; for this reason, I told you that he will take from what is mine and declare it to you. "A little while and you will no longer see me and a little while later you will see me". So, some of his disciple said to one another, "What does this means that he is saying to us, "A little while you will not see me, and again, but a little while you will see me again, because I am going to the father. And they said what is a little while [of which he speaks]? We do not know what he means. Jesus knew their thought and said are you discussing with one another what I said?

Then Jesus said Amen, Amen, you will weep and mourn, while the world rejoices; you will grieve, but your grieve will become joy; When a woman is in labor, She is in anguish because her hour have arrived; But when she has given birth to child, she no longer remembers the pain, because of her joy that a child had been born into the world: So also you are now in anguish. But I will see you again, and your hearts will rejoice, and no one will take your joy from you; on that day, you will ask me about anything: Amen, Amen I say to you; whatever you ask the father in my name he will give to you. Until now you have not asked anything in my name: TO ASK MEANS TO DEMAND: Ask you will receive, so that your joy may be completed: Take courage, I have conquered the world. (John 16:33) I have told you have peace in me, in the world you will trouble, but take courage because I have conquered the world.

CHAPTER 7

In the Beginning was the Word

In the beginning was the word, and the word was with God, and word was God. John 1; 1 He was in the beginning with God. All things came to be through him, and without him nothing came to be. What came to be through him was life, and this life was the light of the human race; the light shines in the darkness, and the darkness has not overcome it. A man named John was sent from God. He came for testimony, to testify to the light, so that all might believe through him. He was not the light, but came to testify to the light. The true light, which enlightens everyone, was coming into the world. He was in the world, and the world became to be through him, but the world did not know him. He came to what was his own, but his own did not accept him. But to those who accept him he gave power to become children of God, to those who believe in his name, who were born not by natural generation nor by human choice nor by man's decision but of God.

And the word became flesh and made his dwelling among us, and we saw his glory, the glory of the father only son, full of grace and truth: John testified to him and cried out, saying,

"This was of whom I said, "The one who is coming after me ranks ahead of me because he existed before me." **From his fullness we have all received, grace in place of grace, because while the law was given through Moses, grace and truth came through Jesus Christ:** No one has ever seen God. The only Son, God, who is at the Father's side, revealed him. And this is the testimony of John. When, the Jews from Jerusalem, sent priest and Levites to him, to ask him, "Who are you?" he admitted, and did not deny it, but admitted," I am not the Messiah." So, they ask him, what are you then? Are you Elijah? And he said, "I am not. Are you the Prophet? He answered no. So, they said to him who are you? So, we can give an answer to those who sent us? **"I am the voice of one crying out in the desert, make straight the way of the Lord:** Isaiah the prophet said, some Pharisees, were also sent. They asked him, "Why then do you Baptist, if you are not the Messiah or Elijah or the prophet? John answered them, I baptize with water, but there is one among you, whom you do not recognize, the one who is coming after me, whose sandal strap I am not worthy to untie. This happened in Bethany across the Jordan, where John was baptizing. The next day he saw Jesus coming towards him and said, "Behold the Lamb of God, who takes the sins of the world. Is the one of whom I said, a man is coming after me who ranks ahead of me because he existed before me. I did not know him, but the reason why I came baptizing with water was that he might be made known to Israel. John testified further, I saw the Spirit come down like a dove from sky and remain upon him. I did not know him, but the one who sent me to baptize with water told me, on whom the Spirit come down and remain, he is the one, **who will baptize you with the holy ghost and fire.** Now I have seen and testified that he is the Son of God. Roman chapter 4 verses 17—18 as it is written "I have made you a father of many nations" in the presence of him whom he believed—God, who gives life to the dead and calls those things which do not exist as though they did; Who contrary to hope, in hope believed, so that he became the father of many nations, according to what was spoken, "So shall your descendants be."

When government officials persecuted Daniel; the book of Daniel Chapter 6 verses 1-28; King Darius decided to appoint a hundred and twenty governors to hold office throughout his empire. In addition, he chose Daniel and two others to supervise the governors and to look after the king's interests. Daniel soon showed that he could do better work than the other supervisors or the governors. Because he was so outstanding, the king considered putting in charge of the whole empire. Then the other supervisor and governors tried to find something wrong with the way Daniel administered the empire, but they couldn't, because Daniel was reliable and did not do anything wrong or dishonest. They said to each other, "We are not going to find anything of which to accuse Daniel unless it is something in connection to his religion."

So, they went to see the king and said, "King Darius may your Majesty live forever. All of us who administers your empire—the supervisors, the governors, the lieutenant governors, and the other officials—have agreed that your Majesty should issue an order and enforce it strictly. Give orders that for thirty days no one be permitted to request anything from any god or any human being except from your Majesty. Anyone who violates this order is to be thrown into a pit filled of lions. So, let your Majesty issues this order and signs it, and it will be a force, a law of the Medes and Persians, which cannot be changed. And so king Darius signed the order. When Daniel learned that the order had been signed, he went home. In an upstairs room of his house there were windows that faced Jerusalem. There, just as he had always done, he knelt down at the open windows and prayed to God three times a day. When Daniel's enemies observed him praying to God, all of them went together to the king to accuse Daniel. They said, "Your Majesty, you signed an order that for the next thirty days anyone who requested anything from any god or from any human being except you would be thrown into a pit filled with lions. The king replied, "Yes, a law of the Medes and Persians, which cannot be changed." Then they said to the king, Daniel, one of the exiles from Judah, does not respect your Majesty, or obey the order you issued. He prays regularly three times a day." When the king heard this, he was upset and did his best to rescue Daniel. He kept trying until sunset. Then Daniel's enemies came back to the king and said to him, "Your Majesty, knows that according to the laws of Medes and Persians no orders which the king's issues can be changed." So, the king gave orders for Daniel to be thrown into the pit filled with lions. He said to Daniel, "May your God, whom who serve so loyally, rescue you." A stone was put over the month of the pit, and the king placed his own royal seal and the seal of his noblemen on the stone, so that no one could rescue Daniel. Then the king returned to the palace and spent sleepless night, without any food or any form of entertainment. At the dawn, the king got up early and hurried to the pit. When he got there, he called out anxiously, "Daniel, servant of the living God. Was your God whom you serve so loyally able to save you from the lions?" Daniel answered, "May your Majesty live forever. God sent his angels to shut the month of the lions so that they would not hurt me. He did this, because he knew that, I was innocent and because I have not wronged you, Your Majesty." The king was overjoyed and gave orders for Daniel to be pulled up out of the pit. So, they pulled him out of the pit, and saw that he had not been hurt at all, for he trusted God. Then the king gave orders to arrest all those who had accused Daniel, and he had them thrown, together with their wives and children, into the pit filled with lions. Before they even reached the bottom of the pit, the lions pounced on them and broke all their bones. Then the king wrote to the people of all nations, races, and languages on earth: "Greetings; I command that throughout my empire everyone should fear and respect the God of Daniel. "He is a living God, and he will rule forever. His kingdom will never be destroyed, and his power will never come to an end. He saves, and rescues; he performs wonders and miracles in heaven and on earth. He saved Daniel from being killed by the lions." Daniel prospered during the reign of Darius and the reign of Cyrus the Persian.

CHAPTER 8

When Daniel and the 3 Hebrew Boys were Persecuted and Sentenced to Death

When three Hebrew believers were sentenced to death: Daniel Chapter 3: King Nebuchadnezzar made a gold statue ninety-foot-tall and nine feet wide and set it up on the plain of Dura in the province of Babylon. Then he sent messages to the princes, prefects, governors, advisers, counselors, judges, magistrates, and all the provincial officials to come to the dedication of the stature he had set up. When the officials had arrived and were standing before the image king Nebuchadnezzar had set up, a herald shouted out, "People of all races and nations and languages, listen to the king's command." When you hear the sound of the horn, flute, zither, lyre, harp, pipes, and other instruments bow to the ground to worship king Nebuchadnezzar's gold stature.

Anyone who refuses to obey will be immediately thrown into a blazing furnace." So, at the sound of the musical instruments, all the people, whatever their race or nation or language, bowed to the ground and worshiped the stature that king Nebuchadnezzar had set up. But some of the astrologers went to the king and informed on the Jews. They said to king Nebuchadnezzar, "Long live the king. You issued a decree requiring all the people to bow down and worship the gold stature when they hear the sound of the musical instruments." That decree also stated that those who refuse to obey must be thrown into a blazing furnace. But there are some Jews whose names are—Shadrach, Meshach, and Abednego—whom you have put in charge of the province of Babylon. They have defied Your Majesty by refusing to serve your gods or to worship the gold statue you have set up. Then king Nebuchadnezzar flew into a rage and ordered Shadrach, Meshach, and Abednego to be brought before him. When they were brought in, Nebuchadnezzar said to them, "Is it true, Shadrach, Meshach, and Abednego, that you refuse to serve my gods, or to worship the statue I have set up?

I will give you one more chance. If you bow down and worship the statue I have made, when you hear the sound of the musical instrument I have made, all will be well. But if you refuse, you will be thrown immediately into the blazing furnace. What god will be able to rescue you from my power then? Shadrach, Meshach and Abednego replied, "O Nebuchadnezzar, we do not need to defend ourselves before you. If we are thrown into the blazing furnace, the God whom we serve is able to save us. He will rescue us from your power, Your Majesty. But if he doesn't, Your Majesty can be sure that we will never serve your gods or worship the gold statue you have set up.

The three friends were thrown into the blazing furnace: Then Nebuchadnezzar lost his temper, and his face turned red with anger at Shadrach, Meshach and Abednego. So, he ordered the furnace to be heated seven times hotter than usual. And he commanded the strongest men in his army to tie the three men up and throw them into the blazing furnace. So, they tied them up, fully dressed in shirts, robes, caps, and all and threw them into the blazing furnace. Now because the king had given strict orders for the furnace to be made extremely hot, the flames burnt up the guards who took the men into the furnace.

Then Shadrach, Meshach, and Abednego, still tied up, fell into the hearts of the blazing fire; Suddenly Nebuchadnezzar leaped to his feet in amazement. He asked his officials, "Didn't we tie up three men and throw them into the blazing furnace?" They answered, "Yes, we did, Your Majesty." Then why do I see four men walking around in the fire?" he asked. "They are not tied up, and they show no signs of being hurt and the forth one look like an Angel." Then Nebuchadnezzar went up to the door of the blazing furnace and called out, "Shadrach, Meshach, and Abednego, Servants of the Supreme God, Come out. And they came out at once. All the princes, governors, lieutenant governors, and other officials of the king gathered to look at the three men, who had not been harmed by the fire. Their hair was not touched and their clothes were not burned, and there was no smoke on them. The king said, "Praise the God of Shadrach, Meshach, and Abednego. He sent his angels and rescues these men who serve and trust him. They disobeyed my orders and risked their lives rather than bow down and worship any god expect their own. "And now I command that if anyone of any nation or language speaks disrespectfully of the God of Shadrach, Meshach, and Abednego, he is to be torn limb from limb, and his house to be made a pile of ruins. There is no other God who can deliver like this. And the king promoted Shadrach, Meshach, and Abednego to higher positions in the province of Babylon.

CHAPTER 9

When the Spies Brought Evil Report

When the spies brought evil report: Numbers chapter 13; The Lord said to Moses, choose one of the leaders from each of the tribes and sent them as spies to explore the land of Canaan, which I am giving to the Israelites. Moses obeyed and from the wilderness of Paran he sent out twelve leaders among them were Joshua and Caleb. When Moses sent them out, he said to them, "Go north from here into the southern part of the land of Canaan and then on into the hill country. Find out what kind of country it is, how many people live there, and how strong they are. Find out whether the land is good or bad and whether the people live in open place or fortified cities. Find out whether the soil is fertile and whether the land is wooded. And be sure to bring back some of the fruits that grows there." (It was the season when grapes were beginning to ripen.) So the men went north and explored the land from the wilderness of Zin in the south all the way to Rehob, near Hamath Pass in the north. They went first to the southern part of the land and came to Hebron, where the clans of Animan, sheshai, and Tamai, the descendants of a race of gaints called the Anikim, lived. (Hebron was founded seven years before Zoan in Egypt.) They came to Eshcol Valley, and there they cut off a branch which had one bunch of grapes on it so heavy that it took two men to carry it on a pole between them. They also brought some pomegranates and figs. (That place was named Eshcol Valley because of the buanch of grapes the Israelites cut off there.) After exploring the land for forty days, the spies returned to Moses, Aaron, and the whole community of Israel at Kadesh in the wilderness of Paran. They reported what they had seen and showed them the fruits they had brought. They told Moses, "We had explored the land, and found it to be rich and fertile; and here is some of it fruits. But the people who lived there are powerful, and their cities are very large and well-fortified. Even worse we saw the descendants of the giants there. Amalekites live in the southern part of the land, while the Hittites, Jebusites and Amorites live in the hill sides of the country; and Canaanites live by the Mediterranean Sea and along the river Jordan. Caleb silenced the people who were complaining against Moses, and said "We should attack now, and take the land; we are strong enough to conquer it. But the ten men who had gone with Caleb said, "No we are not strong enough to attack them." The people there are more powerful than we are." So they spread a false report among the Israelites about the land they had explored. They said that land didn't even produce enough to feed the people who live there. Everyone we saw was very tall, and we even saw giants there, the descendants of Anak. We felt as small as grasshoppers, and that is how we must have looked to them.

Warning against complaining: All night long the people cried out in distress. They complained against Moses and Aaron, and said, "It would have been better to die in Egypt or even here in the wilderness. Why is the Lord taking us into that land? We will be killed in battle, and our wives and children would be captured. Wouldn't it be better to go back to Egypt? So, they said to one another "lets choose a leader, and go back to Egypt." Then Moses and Aaron bowed to the ground in front of all the people. And Joshua son of Nun and Caleb son of Jephunneh, two of the spies, tore their clothes in sorrow, and said to the people, "The land we explored is an excellent land. If the Lord is pleased with us, he will take us there and give us that rich and fertile land.

Do not rebel against the Lord and don't be afraid of the people who live there. We will conquer them easily. The Lord is with us and has defeated the gods who protected them; so, don't be afraid. The whole community has threatened to stone them to death, but suddenly the people saw the dazzling light of the Lord's presence appear over the tent. **Moses prays for the people:** The Lord said to Moses, "How much longer will these people reject me? How much longer will they refuse to trust in me? Even though I have performed so many miracles among them? I will send an epidemic and destroy them, but I will make you the father of a nation that is larger and more powerful than they are. But Moses said to the Lord, "You brought these people out of Egypt by your power. When the Egyptians hear what you have done to your people, they will tell it to the people who live in this land. These people have already heard that you, Lord, are with us, that you appear in plain sight, when your cloud stops over us, that you go before us, by pillar of cloud by day and pillar of fire by night. Now if you kill all your people, the nations who have heard of your fame will say that you killed your people in the wilderness because you were not able to bring them into the land you promised to give them. So now, Lord I pray, show us your power and do what you promised when you said, I, the Lord, am not easily angered, and I show great love and faithfulness and forgive sin and rebellion.

Yet I will not fail to punish children and grandchildren to the third and fourth generation for the sins of their parents. And now, Lord, according to the greatness of your unchanging love, forgives pray, the sin of these people, just as you have forgiven them ever since they left Egypt. The Lord answered, I will forgive them, as you have asked. "But I promise that as surely as I live and as surely as the earth is fills with my presence, none of these people will live to enter that land. They have seen the dazzling light of my presence and the miracles that I performed in Egypt and in the wilderness, but they have tried my patience over again and have refused to obey me. They will never enter the land which I promised to their ancestors. None of those who rejected me will ever enter it. But because my servants Caleb has a different attitude and has remained loyal to me, I will bring him into the land which he had explored, and his descendants will possess the land in who's Valleys Amalekites and the Canaanites now live. Turn back tomorrow and go into the wilderness in the direction of the Gulf; **The Lord punishes the people for complaining:** The Lord said to Moses and Aaron, "How much longer these people are wicked people going to complain against me? I have had enough of these complaints. Now give them this answer; I swear that as I live, I will do to you just what you have asked.

I, the Lord have spoken. You will die and your corpses will be scattered across this wilderness. Because you have complained against me, none of you over twenty years of age will enter that land, except Joshua and Caleb. You will suffer the consequences of your sins for forty years, one year for each of the forty days you spent exploring the land. The men Moses had sent to explore the land brought back a false report which caused the people to complain against the Lord. And so, the lord struck them with a disease, and they died. Of the twelve spies only, Joshua and Caleb survive.

CHAPTER 10

When the Walls of Jerusalem were Broken

When the walls of Jerusalem were broken down (Ezra chapter 1, 2 and 3): In the first year that Cyrus of Persia was emperor, the Lord made what he had said through the prophet Jerimiah come true. He convicted and prompted and moved the heart of Cyrus to issue the following command and send it out in writing to be read aloud everywhere in his empire: "This is the command of Cyrus, Emperor of Persia. The Lord, the God of Heaven, has made me ruler over the whole world and has given me the responsibly of building a Temple for him in Jerusalem in Judah. May God be with all of you who are his people? You are to go to Jerusalem and rebuild the Temple of the Lord, the God of Israel, and the God who is worshipped in Jerusalem.

If any of his people in exile needs help to return, their neighbors are to give them this help. They are to provide them with silver and gold, suppliers and pack animals, as well as offerings to present in the Temple of God in Jerusalem." Then the heads of the clans of the tribes of Judah and Benjamin, the priest and Levites, and everyone else whose heart God has moved got ready to go and rebuild the Lords Temple in Jerusalem. "All their neighbors helped them by giving them many things: silver utensils, gold, supplies, pack animal and other valuables, and offerings for the Temple. Emperor Cyrus gave them back the bowls and cups that Nebuchadnezzar had taken from the temple in Jerusalem and had put in the Temple of his gods. He handed them over to Mithredath, chief of the royal treasury, who made an inventory of them for Sheshbazzar, the governor of Judah as follows: (a) 30 GOLD BOWLS FOR OFFERINGS (b) 1000 SILVER BOWLS FOR OFFERINGS (c) 29 OTHER BOWLS (d) 30 SMALL GOLD BOWLS (e) 410 SMALL SILVER BOWLS 1000 OTHER UTENSILS; In all there were 5,400 gold and silver bowls and other articles which Sheshbazar took with him when he and the other exiles went from Babylon to Jerusalem. Many of the exiles left the province of Babylon and returned to Jerusalem and Judah, all to their own hometowns. Their families had been living in exile in Babylonia ever since Nebuchadnezzar had taken them there as prisoners. Their leaders were Zerubbabel, Joshua, Nehemiah, Seraiah, Reelaiah, Mordecai, Bilshan, Mispar, Bigvai, Rehum, and Baanah. When the exile arrived at the Lord's Temple in Jerusalem, some of the leaders of the clans gave freewill offerings to help rebuild the Temple on its old sites. They gave as much as they could for this work, and the total came to 1,030 pounds of gold, and 5,740 pounds of silver, and 100robes of priests. The priests, the Levites, and some of the people settled in or near Jerusalem; the musicians, the Temple guards and the Temple workers settled in nearby towns; and the rest of the Israelites settled in the towns where their ancestors had lived. By the seventh months the people of Israel were all settled in their towns.

Then they all assembled in Jerusalem and Joshua son of Jehozadak, his fellow priests, and Zerubbabel son of Shealtiel, together with his relatives, rebuilt the altar of the God of Israel, so that they could burn sacrifices on it according to the instructions written in the Law of Moses, the man of God. Even though the returning exiles were afraid of the people who were living in the land, they rebuilt the altar where it had stood before. Then they began once again to burn on it the regular morning and evening sacrifices. They celebrated the Festival of shelters according to the regulations; each they offered the sacrifices required on that day; and in addition, they offered the regular sacrifices to be burned whole and those to be offered at the New Moon Festival and at all the other regular assemblies at which the Lord is worshipped, as well as all the offerings that were given to the Lord voluntarily. Although the people had not yet started to rebuild the Temple, they began on the first day of the seventh month to burn sacrifices to the Lord. **The rebuilding of the Temple**: the people gave money to pay the stonemasons and the carpenters, and gave food, drink, and olive oil to be sent to the cities of Tyre and Sidon in exchange for cedar trees from Lebanon, which were to be brought by sea to Joppa. All this was done with the permission of Emperor Cyrus of Persia. So in the second month of the year after they came back to the site of the Temple in Jerusalem, they began work. Zerubbabel, Joshua, and the rest of their people, the priests, and Levites, in fact all the exiles who had come back to Jerusalem, joined in the work. All the Levites twenty years of age or older were put in charge of the work of rebuilding the Temple. When the builders started to lay the foundation of the Temple, the priests in their robes took their places with trumpets in their hands, and the Levites of the clan of Asaph stood there with cymbals. They praised the Lord according to the instructions handed down from the time of King David. They sang the Lord's praises, repeating the refrain; "The Lord is good and his love for Israel is eternal."

Everyone shouted with all their might, praising the Lord, because the work on the foundation of the Temple had been started. Many of the older priests, Levites, and heads of clan had seen the first temple, and they watched the foundation of this Temple being laid, they cried and wailed. But the others who were there shouted for joy. No one could distinguish between the joyful shouts and crying, because the noise they made was so loud that it could be heard for miles. **Opposition to the rebuilding of the Temple in Jerusalem: Ezra Chapter 4-7:** WORK OF THE TEMPLE BEGINS AGAIN; Work on Temple had been stopped and had remained at a standstill until the second year of the reign of Emperor Darius of Persia. At that time two prophets, Haggai and Zechariah son of Iddo, began to speak in the name of the God of Israel to the Jews who lived in Judah and Jerusalem. When Zerubbabel son of Shealtiel and Joshua son of Jehozadak heard their messages, they began to rebuild the Temple in Jerusalem, and the two prophets helped them. Almost at once Governor Tattennai of West of Euphrates, Shethar Bozenai, and their fellow officials came to Jerusalem and demanded: "Who gave you orders to build this Temple and equip it?" They also asked for the names of all the men who were helping build the Temple. But God was watching over the Jewish leaders, and the Persian officials decided to take no action until they could write to Emperor Darius and receive a reply. This is the report that they sent to the Emperor: "Emperor Darius, may you rule in peace.

"Your Majesty should know that we went to the province of

Judah and found out that the Temple of the great God is being rebuilt with large stone blocks and with wooden beams set in the wall. The work is being done with great care and is moving ahead steadily. We then asked the leaders of the people to tell us who had given them authority to rebuild the Temple and to equip it. We also asked them of their names so that we could inform you who the leaders of this work are. "They answered, "we are servants of the God of heaven and earth, and we are rebuilding the Temple which was originally built and equipped many years ago by a powerful king of Israel. But because our ancestors made the God of heaven angry, he let them be conquered by king Nebuchadnezzar of Babylon, a king of the Chaldean dynasty. The Temple was destroyed, and the people were taken into exile in Babylonia. Then in the first year of the reign of King Cyrus as emperor of Babylonia, Cyrus issued orders for the Temple to be rebuilt. He restored the gold and silver Temple utensils which Nebuchadnezzar had taken from the Temple in Jerusalem and had placed in the temple in Babylon. Emperor Cyrus turned this utensil over to a man named Sheshbazzar, whom he appointed governor of Judah. The emperor told him to take them and return them to the Temple in Jerusalem, and to rebuild the Temple where it had stood before. So Sheshbazzar came and laid it foundation; construction had continued then until the present time, but it is still not finished.

Now if it please Your Majesty, have a search made to the royal records in Babylon to find whether or not Emperor Cyrus gave orders to this Temple in Jerusalem to be rebuilt, and then inform us what your will is in this matter. "EMPEROR CYRUS ORDER REDISCOVERED." So Emperor Darius issued orders for a search to be made in the royal records that were kept in

Babylon. But it was in the city of Ecbatana in the province of Media that a scroll was found, containing the following record: In the first year of his reign Emperor Cyrus commanded that the Temple in Jerusalem be rebuilt as a place where sacrifices are made and offerings are burned. The Temple is to be ninety feet high and ninety feet wide.

The walls are to be built with one layer of wood on top of each layer of stone. All expenses are to be paid by the royal treasury. Also the gold and silver utensils which king Nebuchadnezzar brought to Babylon from the Temple in Jerusalem are to be returned to their proper place in the Jerusalem Temple. **"Emperor Darius order the work in Jerusalem to continue**: Then Emperor Darius sent the following reply: "To Tattennai, governor of West of Euphrates, Shether Bozenai, and your fellow officials in West of Euphrates. "Stay away from the Temple and do not interfere with its construction. Let the governor of Judah and the Jewish leaders rebuild the Temple of *God where it stood before,* I hereby command you to help them rebuild it.

Their expenses are to be paid promptly out of the royal funds received from taxes in West of Euphrates, so that the work is not interrupted. Day by day, without fail, you are to give the priest in Jerusalem whatever they tell you they need: young bulls. Sheep's or lambs to be burnt as offerings to the God of Heaven, or wheat, or salt, wine, or olive oil. This is to be done so that they can offer sacrifices that are acceptable to the God of Heaven and pray for his blessings on me and my sons. I further command that if any disobey this order, a wooden beam is to be torn out of their houses, sharpened on one end, and then driven through their bodies; And their houses to be made a rubbish heap. May the God who chose Jerusalem as the place where he is to be worshipped overthrow any king or nation that defies this command and tries to destroy the Temple there? I, Darius had commanded. My command must be fully obeyed. **Nehemiah's concern for Jerusalem:** The book of Nehemiah Chapter 1 through 4. This the account of what Nehemiah son of Hacaliah accomplished. In the month of Kislev in the twentieth year that Artaxerxes was emperor of Persia, I, Nehemiah, was in Susa, the capital city. Hanani, one of my brothers, arrived from Judah with another group, and I asked them about Jerusalem and about the other Jews who had returned from exile in Babylonia. They told me that those who had survived and were back in the homeland were in great difficulty and reproach and that the foreigners who lived nearby looked down on them. They also told me that the walls of Jerusalem were still broken down and that the gates had not been restored since the time they were burned. **When I heard all these, I sat down and wept, for several days I moaned and I did not eat, I prayed to God:** Lord God of Heaven; you are great, and we stand in fear of you. You faithfully keep your covenant with those who love you and keep your command. Look at me, Lord, and hear my prayer, as I prayed day and night for your servants, the people of Israel. I confess that we, the people of Israel have sinned. My ancestors and I have sinned. We have acted wickedly against you and have not done what you have commanded. We have not kept the laws which you gave us through Moses, your servant. Remember now what you told Moses: "If you people of Israel are unfaithful to me, I will scatter you among the other nations. But if you turn back to me, and do what I have commanded you, I will bring you back to the place where I have chosen to be worshipped, though you were scattered to the ends of the earth. "Lord these are your servants, your own people. You rescue them by your own power and strength. Listen now to my prayers and to the prayers of all your other servants who want to honor you. Give me success today and make the emperor merciful to me." In those days I was the emperor's wine steward. Nehemiah's goes to Jerusalem; One day four months later; when emperor Artaxerxes was dinning, I took the wine to him. He never had seen me look sad before, so he asked, "Why are you looking so sad? You aren't sick, so it must be that are unhappy." I was startled and I answered, "May your Majesty live forever. How can I keep from looking sad when the city where my ancestors are buried is in ruins and its gates had been destroyed by fire?" The emperor asked, "What is it that you want?" I prayed to God of Heaven, and then I said to the emperor, "If Your Majesty is pleased with me and is willing to grant me request, let me go to the land of Judah, to the city where my ancestors are buried, so that I can rebuild the city." The emperor, with the empress sitting at his right side, approved my request. God speaks to you through dreams. Daniel Chapter 4 and 5: King Nebuchadnezzar sent the following message to the people of all nations, races, and languages in the world: "Greetings; listen to my account of the wonders and miracles which the Supreme God has shown me. "How great are the wonders God showed us; how powerful are the miracles he performs; God is king forever; he will rule for all time. I was living comfortably in my palace, enjoying great prosperity. But I had a frightening dream and I saw terrifying visions while I was asleep. I ordered all the royal advisers in Babylon to be brought to me so that they could tell me what the dream meant. Then all the fortunetellers, magicians, wizards, and astrologers were brought in, and *then I told them my dream, but they could not* explain it to me.

Then Daniel came in. (He is also called Belteshazzar, after the name of my god.) The spirit of the holy God is in him, so I told him what I had dreamed. I said to him; Belteshazzar, chief of the fortunetellers, I know that the spirit of the holy God is in you and that you understand all mysteries. This is my dream. Tell me what it means. "While I was asleep, I had a vision of huge tree in the middle of the earth. It grew bigger and bigger until it reached the sky and could be seen by everyone in the world. Its leaves were beautiful, and it was loaded down with fruits—enough for the whole world to eat. Wild animals rested in its shade, birds-built nests in its branches, and every kind of living being ate its fruits. While I was thinking about the vision, I saw coming down from heaven an angel, alert and watchful. He proclaimed in a loud voice, "Cut the tree down, and chop off its branches; strip off its leaves and scatter its fruits. Drive the animals from under it and the birds out of its branches. But leave the stump in the ground with a band of iron and bronze around it. Leave it there in the field with grass. "Now let the dew now fall on this man and let him live with the animals and the plants. For seven years he will not have a human mind, but the mind of an animal. This is the decision of the alert and watchful angels. So then, let all people everywhere know that the Supreme God has power over human kingdoms and he can give them to anyone he chooses—even to those who are least important. "This is the dream I had, "said king Nebuchadnezzar. "Now, Belteshazzar, tell me what it means. None of my royal advisers could tell me, but you can, because the spirit of the holy God is in you." DANIEL EXPLAINS THE DREAM; at this, Daniel, who is also called Belteshazzar, was so alarmed that he could not say anything. The king said to him, "Belteshazzar, don't let the dream and its message alarm you." Belteshazzar replied,

Your Majesty, I wish that the dream and its explanation applied to your enemies and not to you. The tree, so tall that it's reached the sky, could be seen by everyone in the world. Its leaves were beautiful, and it had enough fruit on it to feed the whole world. Wild animals rested under it, and birds made their nests in its branches. Your Majesty, you are the tree, tall and strong. You have grown so great that you reach the sky, and your power extends over the whole world. While your Majesty was watching an angel came down from heaven and said, "Cut tree down and destroy it, but leave the stump in the ground. Wrap a band of iron and bronze around it and leave it there in the field with the grass. Let the dew fall on this man and let him lives there with the animals for seven years. This, then, is what it means your Majesty, and this is what the Supreme God has declared will happen to you.

You will be driven away from human society and you will live with wild animals. For seven years you will eat grass like an ox and sleep in open space where the dew will fall on you. Then you will admit that the Supreme God controls all human kingdoms and that he can give them to anyone he chooses. The angel ordered the stump to be left in the ground. This means that you will become king again when you acknowledge that God rules the entire world. So then, your Majesty follows my advice. Stop sinning, do what is right, and BE MERCIFUL TO THE POOR; then you will continue to be prosperous. All these did happen to Nebuchadnezzar. Only twelve months later, while he was walking around on the roof of his royal palace in Babylon, he said, "Look how great Babylon is, I built it as my capital city to display my power and might, my glory and Majesty." Before the words were out of his mouth, a voice spoke from heaven, "king Nebuchadnezzar listen to what I say. Your royal power is now taken away from you. You will be driven away from human society, live with wild animals, and eat grass like an ox for seven years. Then you will acknowledge that the Supreme God has power over human kingdoms and that he can give them to anyone he chooses. The words came true immediately. Nebuchadnezzar was driven out of human society and ate grass like an ox. The dew fell on his body, and his hair grew as long as eagle feathers and his nails as long as bird claws. When seven years had passed, said the king, "I looked up at the sky, and my sanity returned. I praised the Supreme God and gave honor and glory to the one who lives forever. He will rule forever, and his kingdom will last for all time. He looks on the people of the earth as nothing; angels in heaven and people on earth are under his control. No one can oppose his will or question what he does. When my sanity returned, my honor and glory, and Majesty and the glory of my kingdom were given back to me. My officials and noblemen welcomed me, and I was given back my royal power with even greater honor than before. And now, I, Nebuchadnezzar, praise, honor, and glorify the king of Heaven. Everything he does is right and just, and he can humble anyone who acts proudly.

Pride goes before a fall; Belshazzar the son of king Nebuchadnezzar: Daniel Chapter 5; One-night king Belshazzar invited a thousand noblemen to a great banquet, and they drank wine together. While they were drinking, Belshazzar gave orders to bring in the gold and silver cups and bowls which his father Nebuchadnezzar had carried off from the Temple in Jerusalem. The king sent for them so that he, his noblemen, his wives, and his concubines could drink out of them. At once the gold cups and bowls were brought in, and they all drank wine out of them and praised gods made of gold, silver, bronze, iron, wood and stone.

Suddenly a human hand appeared and began writing on the plaster wall of the palace, where the light from the lamps was shining most brightly. And the king saw the hand as it was writing. He turned pale and was so frightened that his knees began to shake. He shouted for someone to bring in the magicians, wizards, and astrologers. When they came in, the king said to them, "Anyone who can read this writing and tell me what it means will be dressed in robes of royal purple, wear a gold chain of honor around his neck, and be the third in power in the kingdom. The royal advisers came forward, but none of them could read the writing or tell the king what it meant. In his distress king Belshazzar grew even paler, and his noblemen had no idea what to do. The queen mother heard the noise made by the king and his noblemen and entered the banquet hall. "May your Majesty live forever, please do not be disturbed and look so pale. There is a man in your kingdom that has the spirit of the holy God in him. When your father was king, this man showed good sense, knowledge, and wisdom like the wisdom of the gods. And king Nebuchadnezzar, your father, made him chief of the fortunetellers, magicians, wizards and astrologers. He has unusual ability and is wise and skillful in interpreting dreams, solving riddles, and explaining mysteries; so, send for this man Daniel, whom the king named Belteshazzar, and he will tell you what all this means.

Daniel was brought at once into the king's presence, and the king said to him, "Are you Daniel, that Jewish exile, whom my father the king brought here from Judah? I have heard that the spirit of the holy God is in you and that you are skillful and have knowledge and wisdom. The advisers and magicians were brought in to read this writing and tell me what it means, but they could not discover the meaning. Now I have heard that you can find hidden meanings and explain mysteries. If you can read this writing and tell me what it means, you will be dressed in a rope of royal purple, wear a gold chain of honor around your neck, and be the third in power in the kingdom. "Daniel replied keep your gifts for yourself or give them to someone else. I will read for your Majesty what has been written and tell you what it means. The Supreme God made your father Nebuchadnezzar a great king and gave him dignity and Majesty. He was so great that people of all nations, races, and languages were afraid of him and trembled. If he wanted to kill someone, he did; if he wanted to keep someone alive, he did; He honored and disgraced anyone he wanted to. But because he became proud, stubborn, and cruel, he was removed from his royal throne and lost his place of honor. He was driven away from human society, and his mind became like that of an animal. He lived with wild donkeys, ate grass like an ox, and slept in the open air with nothing to protect him from the dew. Finally, he admitted that the Supreme God controls all human kingdoms and can give them to anyone he chooses.

But you, his son, have not humbled yourself, even though you knew all this. You acted against the Lord of Heaven and brought in the cups and bowls taken from his Temple. You, your noblemen, your wives, and your concubines drank wine out of them, and praised the gods made of gold, silver, bronze, iron, wood, and stone—gods that cannot see or hear and that do not know anything. But you did not honor the

God who determines whether you live or die and who controls everything you do. That is why God has sent the hand to write these words. This is what was written: Number, Number, weight, divisions. And this is what it means; number, God has numbered the days of your kingdom and brought it to an end; weight, you have been weighed on the scales and found to be too light; divisions, your kingdom is divided up and given to the Medes and Persians." Immediately Belshazzar ordered his servants to dress Daniel in a rope of royal purple and to hang a gold chain of honor around his neck. And he made him the third in power in the kingdom. That same night Belshazzar, the king of Babylonia, was killed; and Darrius the Mede, who was then sixty-two years old, seized the royal power.

A revolution: Revolt (disambiguation)

A Revolution from the Latin revolution, ("a turnaround") is a fundamental change in power or organizational structures that take place in a relatively short period of time. Aristotle described two types of political revolution: A complete change from one constitution to another; Modification of an existing constitution. Revolutions have occurred through human history and vary widely in terms of methods, duration, and motivating ideology. Their results include major changes in culture, economy, and social-political institution.

CHAPTER 11

The Revolutionary Acts of Courage by Ordinary People

Mahatma Gandhi's salt March to Dandi: Mahatma Gandhi's salt march to Dandi in 1930 alerted the world to the burgeoning Indian independence movement. Gandhi's defiant act was the first campaign against British imperialism since the National Congress declaration of independence earlier that same year. A pioneer in mass non-violent protest ever since his expatriation in South Africa as a young man, Gandhi chose to defy the British salt laws by organizing a 248-mile trek to a coastal town illegally make salt from the sea. By the time he and his thousands of followers reached the sea, word had spread across the country and millions of impoverished and malcontented Indians took up the civil disobedience by disregarding the salt laws. While Gandhi's march did not directly bring about national independence, it was vital in turning world opinion against British policies in India. For his long-life struggle for freedom, Gandhi is immortalized as the nation's founding father and remains one of the world's most beloved figures.

Rosa Park's sit down civil rights: Popularly remembered as the woman who quietly refused to give up her seat for a white passenger on a segregated bus, thereby launching the civil rights movement, Rosa Parks was already steeped in black politics long before her iconic arrest. A secretary of the Montgomery chapter of the NAACP since 1943, she was well aware of the group's attempts to challenge the Jim Crow laws on public transportation and supported their plans to instigate a bus boycott. Rosa Parks reputes the common myth that her unwillingness to get up was due to aching feet. "No, she said, "the only tired I was, was tired of giving in." Although instrumental to the Civil Rights movement, Parks went to live in anonymity after the protests, working as a seamstress for almost a decade and not receiving national recognition until later in life. **Aung San Suu Kyi and Freedom from fear:** Aung San Suu Kyi came from a prominent political background-her father helped liberate Burma from British Colonial control after WW11 and her mother was the fledging nation's ambassador to India. Spending most of her younger adult years studying and raising a family abroad, Aung San Suu Kyi always felt that the time might come to take up her family's legacy and fight the oppressive military dictatorship that had overthrown the civilian government initiated by her father. That moment came when Aung San Suu Kyi returned to Burma in 1988 to care for her ailing mother. Her visit coincides massive public demonstrations against the junta, and she joined the fray. Emerging as the most compelling leader of the popular revolt, Aung San Suu Kyi helped found an opposition political party, the National League Democracy. In 1990, she was voted in as Prime Minister in the first multi-party elections-triumph that was nullified by the military government, which had already placed her under house arrest. When the junta offered her release in exchange for permanent exile, Aung San Suu Kyi refused. Instead the courageous and principled leader continues to live in house arrest, despite the constant peril to her life and decades long separation from her family. Aung San Suu Kyi tenacious dedication to see a better Burma has led to countless international awards, including the Nobel Peace Prize.

Martin Luther King Jr. I have a dream speech; one of the finest orators and civil rights leaders of the 20th century, Martin Luther king, Jr. did much to change the United States policy on racial discrimination. After helping to launch the civil rights movements by heading the 1955 Montgomery Bus Boycott, king founded the southern Christian leadership conference, a black religious organization that directed nonviolent protests against segregationist authorities throughout the 1960s. The zenith of Dr. King's career came on august 28, 1963 with his "I have a dream" speech, given at the march on Washington for Jobs and Freedom. On the symbolic steps of the Lincoln Memorial, king spoke to 200,000-300,000 dissidents and millions of television viewers, rallying for a world free of prejudice in which people would not be judged by the color of their skin, but by the content of their character." Dr. King's historical speech was major deciding factor in the passage of the National Voting Act and Civil Rights Acts. For his part in advocating racial harmony and equality through nonviolent means, King became the youngest ever to receive the Nobel Peace Prize in 1964. Although as an assassin lamentably cut his momentous career short in 1968, Martin Luther king, Jr. and his words continue to inspire the oppressed everywhere.

Challenge for women's right movement: Women rights

movements are primarily concerned with making the political, social, and economic status of women equal to that
of men and with establishing legislative safeguards against
discrimination on the basis of gender. Women's rights movements have worked in support of these aims for more than
two centuries. They date to at least the first feminist publication, in 1792, entitled A Vindication of the Rights of Women,
by British writer Mary Wollstonecraft. Militant political action
among women began in Britain in 1903 with the information
of the women's social and political Union (WSPU) for the
rights to vote.

The Organization was led by Emmeline Pankhurst. Women
of all ages and classes demonstrated on a massive scale;
the demonstrators were jailed, locked out of their meetings
places, and thrown down the steps of parliaments. Nation di-
visiveness ended in a truce at the outbreak of the World War
1 (1914) with the WSPU's decision to support the war effort.
The ensuring mobilization by the WSPU of thousands of its
members for voluntary participation in the war industries and
support services was highly influential factor in overcoming
government resistance to WSPU aims. The right to vote was
granted in 1918; it was confined to women age 30 and above.
In 1928 the voting age was lowered to 21. In the United
States, the first definitive position on women's right—hitherto
intermingled with antislavery issues—was taken in 1848 under the leadership of Queen Cady Stanton at the Women's
Rights Convention at Seneca Falls N. Y.(see Seneca Falls
Convention). In 1850 the National Women Rights Convention
was held, led by Lucy Stone, an elderly activist. Both groups
coalesced in the formation (1863) of the Women's National
Loyal League, under Susan B. Anthony. Anthony wrote and

submitted in 1878 a proposed right-to-vote amendment to the Constitution. In 1890, Wyoming became the first state with women's suffrage. The movement was accelerated by the formation (1890) of the National American Women's Suffrage Association and the election (1990) of Carrie Chapman Catt as president.

The ensuring campaign attracted many educated, wealthy, and influential women to the cause, with resultant political professionalism, increased funding, and the developments of massive parades and demonstrations in the major cities. The Anthony amendment, as written in 1878, was ratified as the 19th Amendment and became law in 1920. From 1920 to 1960, militancy on behalf of single issues diffused into a number of women's political groups, such as the League of Women Voters (1920) and the National Council of Negros Women (1935). Such groups supported various types of liberal reforms related to the rights of both men and women. An equal rights amendment drafted in 1923 by the National Women's party (founded 1913) remained dormant for another 50 years. At the international level, however, the women's right movement made progress.

CHAPTER 12

American Revolution: The Colonists

In this article, inhabitants of the Thirteen Colonies who supported the American Revolution are primarily referred to as "American" or "Patriots" and sometimes as "Whigs" Rebels" or "Revolutionaries." Colonists who supported the British side are called "Loyalists" or "Tories." In British English, these events are known as "American War of Independence." The American Revolution was a political upheaval that took place between 1765 and 1783 during which rebels in the Thirteen American Colonies rejected monarchy and aristocracy in a revolutionary move, overthrew the authority of Britain, and founded the United States of America.

The American Revolution was the result of a series of social, political, and intellectual transformations in American society, government and the ways of thinking. Starting in 1765 the Americans rejected the authority of the British parliament to tax them; protests continued to escalate, as in the Boston Tea Party of 1773, and the British responded by imposing punitive laws—the Coercive Acts—on Massachusetts in 1774. The other colonies rallied behind Massachusetts and set up Congress to take charge. The Patriots fought the British and loyalists in the American Revolutionary war (1775-1783). Formal acts of rebellion against British authority began in 1774 when the Patriot Suffolk Resolves effectively replaced the royal government of Massachusetts, and confined British control to the city of Boston. Tensions escalated to the outbreak of fighting between Patriot militia and British regulars at the Lexington and Concord in April 1775. Patriots in each of the thirteen colonies formed a Provincial Congress that usurped power from the old colonial government and suppressed loyalism. Resistance to the British was coordinated through the Second Continental Congress. Claiming King George 111's rule was tyrannical and violated the rights of Englishmen. The Continental Congress declared the colonies free and independent states in July 1776. These thirteen states became known as the United States of America, a loose confederacy under the 1777 Articles of Confederation.

The Patriot leadership professed the political philosophies of liberalism and republicanism to reject monarchy and aristocracy and proclaimed that all men are created equal. Congress rejected the proposals for compromise that would keep them under the king. The British were forced out of Boston in 1776, but then captured and held New York City for the duration of the war, nearly capturing General Washington and his army. The British blockade the ports and captured other cities for brief periods but failed to defeat Washington's forces. In early 1778, after an invading British army from Canada was captured by the Americans, the French entered the war as allies of the United States. The Naval and military power of the two sides were about equal, and France had allies in the Netherlands and Spain: while Britain had no major allies in this large scale war. The war later turned to the American South, where the British captured an army at South Carolina, but failed to enlist enough volunteers from Loyalist civilians to take effect control. A combined American—French force captured a second British army at Yorktown in 1781, effectively ending the war in the United States. A peace treaty in 1783 confirmed the new nation's complete separation from the British Empire. The United States took possession of nearly all the territory east of Mississippi River and south of the Great Lakes, with the British retaining control of Canada and Spain taking Florida.

Among the significant results of the revolution was the creation of a democratically-elected representative government responsible to the will of the people. The period after the peace treaty came in 1783 involved debates between nationally-minded men like Washington who wanted a strong national government, and the leaders who wanted strong states but weak national government. The former group won the ratification of the new United States Constitution in 1788. It replaced the weaker Articles of Confederation and Perpetual Union. The new Constitution established a relatively strong federal national government that included a strong elected president, national courts, a bicameral Congress that represented both the states in the Senate and population in the House of Representatives. Congress has powers of taxation that were lacking under the old Articles. The United States Bill of Rights of 1791 comprised the ten amendments to the Constitution, guaranteeing many "natural rights" that were influential in justifying the revolution, and attempted to balance a strong national government with strong states governments and broad personal liberties. The American shift to liberal republicanism, and the gradually increasing democracy, caused an upheaval of traditional social hierarchy and gave birth to the ethic that has formed a core of political values in the Unites States.

CHAPTER 13

Job Turned Adversity into Opportunity and Victory

There was a man called Job, living in the land of Uz, who worshipped God and was faithful to him. He was a good man, careful not to do anything evil. He had seven sons and three daughters, and owned seven thousand sheep, three thousand camels, one thousand head of cattle, and five hundred donkeys. He also had a large number of servants and was the richest man in the East. Job's sons used to take turns giving a feast, to which all the other would come, and they always invited their three sisters to join them. The morning after each feast, Job would get up early and offer sacrifices for each of his children in order to purify them.

He always did this because he thought one of them might have sinned by insulting God unintentionally. When the day came for the heavenly being to appear before the Lord, Satan was there among them. The Lord asked him, what have been doing? Satan answered; I have been walking here and there, roaming around the earth. Did you notice my servant Job? The

Lord asked. There is no one on earth as faithful and good as he is. He worshipped me and he is careful not to do anything evil. Satan replied would Job worship you if he got nothing out of it? You have always protected him and his family and everything he owns. You bless everything he does, and you have given him enough cattle to feed the whole country. But now suppose you take everything he has—he will curse you to your face.

Alright, the Lord said to Satan, everything he has is in your power, but you must not hurt Job himself. So, Satan left. One day when Job's children were having a feast at the home of their oldest brother, a massager came running to Job. We were plowing the fields with the oxen, he said and the donkeys were in a nearby pasture. Suddenly the Sabeans attacked and stole them all. They killed every one of your servants except me. I am the only one who escaped to tell you. Before he had finished speaking, another servant came and said, Lighting struck the sheep and the shepherd and killed them all. I am the only one who escaped and came to tell you. Before he had finished another servant came and said, the bands of Chaldean raiders attacked us, and took away the camels, and killed all your servants except me. I am the only one who escaped to tell you. Before he had finish speaking, another servant came and said, your children were having a feast bin the home of your oldest son, when a storm swept in from the desert. It blew the house down and killed them all. I am only one who had escaped to tell you. Then Job got up and tore his clothes in grief, He shaved his head and threw himself face downward on the ground. He said, I was born with nothing, and I will die with nothing. The Lord gave and now he had taken away. May his name be praised? In spite of everything that has happened, Job did not sin by blaming God. Job 2 When the day came for the heavenly beings to appear before the Lord again, Satan was there among them. The Lord asked him, where have you been? Satan answered; I have been walking here and there, roaming around the earth. Did you notice my servants Job? The Lord asked, there is no one on earth as faithful and good as he is. He worships me and is careful not to do anything evil. You persuaded me to let you attacks him for no reason at all, but Job is still as faithful as ever. Satan replied, **"A person will give up everything in order to stay alive":** Job 2;4-6 But now suppose you hurt his body—he will curse you to your face. So, the Lord said to Satan, **"All right he is in your power, but you are not to kill him:** Then Satan left the Lord's presence and made sores break out all over Job's body. Job went and sat by the garbage dump and took a piece of broken pottery to scrape his sores. His wife said to him, "You are still as faithful as ever, aren't you? Why don't you curse God and die? Job answered, "You talking nonsense. When God send us something good, we welcome it. How can we complain when he sends us trouble? Even in all the sufferings Job said nothing evil against God.

The all—powerful God; Then Job answered the Lord. I know, Lord, that you are all-powerful; that you can do everything you want. You ask how I dare question your wisdom when I was so very ignorant. I talked about things I did not understand, about marvels too great for me to know. You told me to listen while you spoke and to try to answer your questions. In the past, I knew only what others had told me, but now I have seen you with my own eyes. So, I am ashamed of all I have said and repeat in dust and ashes. After the Lord had finished speaking to Job, he said to Eliphaz I am angry with you and your two friends, because you did not speak the truth about me, the way my servant Job did. Now take seven bulls and seven rams to Job and offer them as a sacrifice for yourselves.

Job will pray for you, and I will answer his prayer and not disgrace you the way you deserve. You did not speak the truth about me as he did. Eliphaz, Bildad, and Zophar did what the Lord had told them to do, and the Lord answered Job prayer. Then, after Job had prayed for his three friends, the Lord made him prosperous again and gave him twice as much as he had had before. All Job's brothers and sisters and former friends came to visit him and feasted with him in the house. They expressed their sympathy and comforted him for all the troubles he Lord had brought upon him. Each of them gave him some money and a gold ring. The Lord blessed the last part of Job's life even more than he had blessed at first. Job owned fourteen thousand sheep, six thousand camels, two thousand head of cattle, and one thousand donkeys. He was the father of seven sons and three daughters. He called the oldest daughter Jemimah, the second Keziah, and the youngest Karen Happuch. There were no women in the whole world as beautiful as Job's daughters. Their father gave a share of the inheritance along with their brothers. Job lived a hundred and forty years after this, long enough to see his grandchildren and great-grandchildren. And he died at a very great age.

You are the light of the world: Listen to me, distant nations, you people who live far away. Before I was born, the Lord chose me and appointed me to be his servant. He made my words as sharp as a sword. With his own hand, he protected me. He made me like an arrow, sharp and ready for use. He said to me, Israel, "you are my servants; because of you people will praise me. I said, "I have worked, but how hope-less it is; I have used up my strength but have accomplished nothing. "Yet I can trust the Lord to defend my cause; he will reward me for what I do. Before I was born, the Lord ap-pointed me; he made me his servant to bring back his people, to bring back the scattered people of Israel. The Lord gives me honor; he is the source of my strength.

The Lord said to me, "I have a greater task for you, my servant. Not only will you restore to greatness the people of Israel who have survived, but I will also make you the light of the world, so that the entire world will be saved. Israel's Holy God and Savior says to the one who is deeply despised, who is hated by the nations and is the servants to the rulers; "Kings will see you released and will rise up to show their respect; princes also will see it, and they will bow low to honor you." This will happen because he Lord had chosen his servants; the holy God of Israel keeps his promises. **RESTORATION OF JERUSALEM;** The Lord says to his people, "When the times comes to save you, I will show you favor and answered your cries for help. I will guard and protect you and through you make a covenant with all peoples, I will let you settle once again in your land that is now laid waste. I will say to the prisoners, Go free; and to those in darkness come out to the light. They will be like sheep that graze on the hills, they will never be hungry or thirsty, Sun and Desert heat will not hurt them, for they will be led by the one who loves them. He will lead them to springs of water. I will make a highway across the mountains and prepare a road for my people to travel. My people will come from far away, from the north and the west, and from Aswan in the south. Sing, heavens; Shout for joy, earth. Let the mountains burst into song. The Lord will comfort his people; he will have pity on his suffering people. But the people of Jerusalem said,

"The Lord has abandoned us; He has forgotten us." So the Lord answered, "Can a woman forget her own baby and not love the child she bore? Even if a mother should forget her child, I will never forget you; I have written your name on the palms of my hands. "Those who will rebuild you are coming soon, and those who destroy you will leave. Look around and see what is happening. Your people are assembling—they are coming home. As surely as I am the living God, you will be proud of your people, as proud as a bride is of her jewels. "Your country was ruined and desolate but now it will be too small for those who are coming to live there. And those who left you in ruins will be far removed from you. Your people who were born in exile will one day say to you, "This land is too small—we need more room to live in. Then you will say to yourself, who bore all these children for me? I lost my children and could have no more. I was exiled and driven away—who brought these children up? I was left alone where did these children come from? The Sovereign Lord says to his people; "I will signal to the nations, and they will bring your children home. Kings will be like fathers to you; queens will be like mothers. They will bow low before you and honor you; they will humbly show their respect for you. Then you will know that I am the lord; no one who waits for my help shall be disappointed." Can you take away a soldier's loot? Can you rescue the prisoners of a tyrant? The lord replies, "That is just what is going to happen. The soldier's prisoners will be taken away and the tyrant's loot will be seized. I will fight against whoever fights you, and I will rescue your children. I will make your oppressors kill each other; they will be drunk with murder and rage. Then all people will know that I am the Lord, the one who saves you and set you free. They will know that I am Israel powerful God."

There is hope for your future: Isaiah 60: Arise, Jerusalem, and shine like the sun; the glory of the Lord is shining on you. Other nations will be covered by darkness, but on you the light of the Lord shall shine; the brightness of his presence will be with you. Nations will be drawn to your light, and kings to the dawning of your new day. Look around you and see what is happening; your people are gathering to come home; your sons will come from far away; your daughters will be carried like children. You will see this and fill of joy; you will tremble with excitement. The wealth of the nations will be brought to you; from across the sea their riches will come. Great caravans of camels will come, from Midian and Ephah. They will come from Sheba, bringing gold and incense.

People will tell the good news of what the Lord had done. All the sheep of Kedar and Nebaioth will be brought to you as a Sacrifice, and shall be offered on the altar to please the Lord. The Lord will make his temple more glorious than ever. What are these ships that skim along like clouds, like doves returning home? They are ships coming from distant lands, bringing God's people home. They bring with them silver and gold to honor the name of the Lord, the holy God of Israel, who has made all nations honor his people. The Lord says to Jerusalem, "Foreigners will rebuild your walls, and their kings will serve you. In my anger I punished you, but now I will show you my favor and mercy. Day and night your gates will be open, so that the kings of the nations may bring you their wealth. But nations that do not serve you will be completely destroyed. The woods of the pine, the juniper, and the cypress, the finest wood from the forests of Lebanon, will be brought to rebuild you, Jerusalem, to make my temple beautiful, to make my city glorious. The descendant of those who oppressed you will come and bow low to show their respect. All who once despised you will worship at your feet. They will call you the "City of the Lord." Zion the City of Israel's holy God. You will no longer be forsaken and hated, A city deserted and desolate. I will make you great and beautiful, a place of joy foever. Nations and kings will care for you as a mother nurses her child. And you will know, I, the Lord have saved you. That the mighty God of Israel sets you free. "I will bring you gold instead of bronze, Silver and bronze instead of iron and woods, and iron instead of stone. Your rulers will no longer oppress you; I will make them rule with justice and peace. The sounds of violence will be heard no more; Destruction will not shatter your family no more. I will protect and defend you like a wall; you will praise me because I have saved you. No longer shall the sun be your light by day or the moon be your light by night; The light of my glory will shine on you. Your days of grief will come to an end. I, the Lord will be your eternal light, more lasting than the sun and the moon. Your people will possess the land.

The good news of liberty: Isaiah 61: The Sovereign Lord has filled me with his Sprit. He has chosen me and sent me to bring good news to the poor, to heal the broken hearted, to announce release to captives and freedom to those in prison. He has sent me to proclaim that the time has come when the Lord will save his people and defeat their enemies. He has sent me to comfort all who mourn, to give to those who mourn in Zion joy and gladness instead of grief, a song of praise instead of sorrow. They will be like trees that the Lord himself has planted. They will all do what is right, and God will be pleased for what he has done. They will rebuild cities that had long been in ruins.

My people, foreigners will serve you. They will take care of your flocks and farm your land and tend your vineyards. And you will be known as the priests of the Lord, the servants of our God; you will enjoy the wealth of the nations and be proud that it is yours. Your shame and disgraced are ended. You will live in your own land. And your wealth will be doubled; your joy will last forever. **Isaiah 62;** I will speak out to encourage you; I will not be silent until you are saved, and your victory shines like a torch in the night. Jerusalem, the nations will see you victorious; all the kings will see your glory. You will be called by a new name, a name given by the Lord himself. You will be like a beautiful crown for the Lord; No longer will you be called "forsaken" or your land be called the deserted wife; your new name will be called "God is pleased with you." Your land will be called "happily married" or "Happiness" because the Lord is pleased with you. And will be like a husband to your land. Like a young man taking a virgin as his bride, He who formed you will marry you. As a groom is delighted with his bride, so your God will delight in you. On your walls, Jerusalem, I have placed sentries (watchmen or intercessors); they must never be silent day or night. They must remind the Lord of his promises and never let him forget them. They must give him no rest until he restores Jerusalem and makes it a city the whole world praise. The Lord has made a solemn promise, and by his power he will carry it out. Your grains will be no longer food for your enemies. And foreigners will no longer drink your wine

CHAPTER 14

When Joseph was Put in Prison

Sometime later the king of Egypt's wine steward and his chief baker offended the king. He was angry with these two officials and put them in prison in the house of the captain of the guard, in the same place where Joseph is being kept. They spent a long time in prison, and the captain assigned Joseph as their servant. One night the wine stewards and the chief baker each had a dream, and the dreams had different meanings. When Joseph came to them in the morning, he saw that they were upset. He asked them, why do you look so worried today? They answered, "Each of us had a dream, and there is no one here to explain the dreams mean." It is God who gives ability to interpret dreams, Joseph said.

"Tell me your dreams." So the wine steward said, "In my dream there was a grapevine in front of me with three branches on it. As soon as the leaves came out, the blossom appeared, and the grapes ripened. I was holding the king's cup; so I took the grapes and squeezed them into the cup and gave it to him. "Joseph said, "this is what it means; the three branches are three days. In three days the king will release you, pardon you, and restore you to your position. You will give him his cup as you did before when you were his wine steward. But please remember me when everything is going well for you, and please be kind enough and mention me to the king and help me get out of this prison. After all, I was kidnapped from the land of the Hebrews, and even here in Egypt I did not do anything wrong to deserve being put in prison. When the chief baker saw the wine steward's dream was favorable, he said to Joseph I had a dream too; I was carrying three bread-baskets on my head. In the top baskets there were all types of baked goods for the king and the birds were eating them." Joseph answered, "This is what it means; the three baskets are three days. In three days the king will release you—and have your head cut off. Then he will hang your body on the pole, and the birds will eat your flesh." On his birthday three days later the king gave a banquet to all his officials; He restored the wine steward to his former position, but he executed the chief baker.

It all happened just like Joseph had said. But the wine steward never gave Joseph another thought—he forgot all about him. **Joseph interprets the king's dream:** After the two years had passed, the king of Egypt dreamed that he was standing by the Nile River, when seven cows, fat and sleek, came up out of the river and began to feed on the grass. Then seven other cows came up; they were thin and bony. They came and stood by the other cows on the riverbank, and the thin cows ate up the fat cows. Then the king woke up. He fell asleep again and had another dream. Seven heads of grain, full and ripe, were growing on one stalk. Then seven other heads of grain sprouted up, thin and scorched by the desert wind, and the thin heads of grain swallowed the full ones. The king woke up and realized that he had been dreaming. In the morning he was worried, so he sent for all the magician and wise men of Egypt. He told them his dreams, but no one could explain them to him. Then the wine steward said to the king, "I must confess today that I have done wrong. You were angry with the chief baker and me, and you put us in prison in the house of the captain of the guard. One night each of us had a dream, and the dreams had different meanings. A young Hebrew was there with us, a slave of the captain of the guard. We told him our dreams, and he interpreted them for us.

Things turned out just as he said: you restored me to my position but you executed the baker." The king sent for Joseph, and he was immediately brought from the prison. After he had shaved and changed his clothes, he came into the king's presence. The king said to him, "I have had a dream, and no one can explain it, I have been told that you can interpret dreams." Joseph answered, "I cannot, Your Majesty, but God will give a favorable interpretation." The kind said, "I dreamed that I was standing on the bank of the Nile, when seven cows, fat and sleek, came up out of the river and began feeding on the grass. Then seven other cows came up which were thin and bony. They were the poorest cows I have ever seen anywhere in Egypt. The thin cows ate up the fat ones, but no one would have known it, because they looked just as bad as before. Then I woke up. I also dreamed that I saw seven heads of grain which were full and ripe, growing on one stalk. Then seven heads of grain sprouted, thin and scorched by the desert wind, and the thin heads of grain swallowed the full ones. I told the dreams to the magicians, but none of them could explain them to me." Joseph said to the king, "The two dreams means the same thing; God has told you what he is going to do. The seven fat cows are seven years, and the seven full heads of grain are also seven years; they have the same meaning. The seven thin cows which came up later and the seven thin heads of grain scorched by the desert wind are seven years of famine.

It is just as I told you—God had shown you what he is going to do. There will be seven years of great plenty in all the land of Egypt. After that, there will be seven years of famine, and all the good years will be forgotten, because the famine will ruin the country. The time of plenty will be entirely forgotten, because the famine which follows will be terrible. The repetition of your dream means that the matter is fixed by God and that he will make it happen in the near future. "Now you should choose some man with wisdom and insight and put him in charge of the country. You must also appoint other officials and take a fifth of the crops during the seven years of plenty. Order them to collect all the food during the good years that are coming, and give them authority to store up in the cities and guard it. The food will be a reserve supply for the country during the seven years of famine which are going to come on Egypt. In this way, the people will not starve." **Joseph is made governor over Egypt:** The king and his officials approved this plan, and he said to them, "We will never find a better man than Joseph, a man who has God's Spirit in him. "The king said to Joseph, "God has shown you all this, so it is obvious that you have greater wisdom and insight than anyone else. I will put you in charge of my country, and all my people will obey your orders. Your authority will be second only to mine. I now appoint you governor over all Egypt.

The king removed from his figure the ring engraved with the

royal seal and put it on Joseph finger. He put a fine linen robe on him, and placed a gold chain around his neck. He gave him the second chariot to ride in, and his guard of honor went ahead of him and cried out, "Make way, Make way. "And so Joseph was appointed governor all over Egypt after the interpretation of the King's dream. The king said to him, "I am the king—and no one in all Egypt shall so much as lift a hand or a foot without your permission." He gave Joseph the Egyptian name Zaphenath Paneah, and he gave him a wife, Asenath, the daughter of Potiphera, a priest in the city of Heliopolis. Joseph was thirty years old when he began to serve the king of Egypt. He left the king's court and travelled all over the land. During the seven years of plenty the land produced abundant crops, of all which Joseph collected and stored in the cities. In each city he stored the food from the fields around it. There was so much grain that Joseph stopped measuring it—it was like the sand of the sea. Before the years of famine came, Joseph had two sons from Asenath. He said God had made me forget all my sufferings and my entire father's family. So he named his first son Manasseh. He also said God had given me children in the land of my trouble"; so named his second son Ephraim. The seven years of plenty that the land of Egypt had enjoyed came to an end, and the seven years of famine began, just as Joseph had said. There was famine in every other country, but there was food throughout Egypt.

When the Egyptians began to be hungry, they cried out to the king for food. So he ordered them to go to Joseph and do what he told them. The famine grew worse and spread over the whole country, so Joseph opened up the store houses and sold grain to the Egyptians. People came to Egypt from all over the world to buy grain because the famine was severe everywhere in the land. **Joseph brothers go to Egypt to buy grains, Genesis Chapter 42:** when Jacob learnt that there was grain in Egypt; he said to his sons, "why don't you do something? I heard that there is grain in Egypt; go there and buy some to keep us from starving to death." So Joseph's ten half-brothers went to buy grain in Egypt, but Jacob did not send Joseph full brother Benjamin with them, because he was afraid that something might happen to him. The sons of Jacob came with others to buy grain, because there was famine in the land of Canaan. Joseph, as governor of the land of Egypt, was selling grain to people from all over the world. So, Joseph's brothers came and bow down before him with their faces to the ground. When Joseph saw his brothers he recognized them, but he acted as if he did not know them. He them harshly, where do you come from?" "We have come from Canaan to buy food, they answered. Although Joseph recognized his brothers, they did not recognize him. He remembered the dreams he had dreamed them and said, "You are spies; you have come to find out where our country is weak.

No, sir, they answered. We have come as your slave to buy food. We are all brothers. We are not spies, sir, we are honest men. "Joseph said to them, no, you have come to find out where the country is weak." They said we are twelve brothers in all, sir, sons of the same man in the land of Canaan. One brother is dead, and the youngest is now with our father. "It is just as said," Joseph answered. "You are spies. This is how you will be tested: I swear by the name of the king that you will never leave until your youngest brother comes here. One of you must go and get him. The rest of you will be kept under guard until the truth of what you say can be tested. Otherwise, as sure as the king lives, you are spies. "With that, put them in prison for three days. On the third day Joseph said to them, I am God-fearing man, and I will spare your lives on one condition. To prove that you are honest, one of you will stay in the prison where you have been kept; the rest of you may go and take back to your starving families the grain that you have bought. Then you must bring your youngest brother to me. This will prove that you have been telling the truth, and I will not put you to Death." They agreed to this and said to one another, "Yes, now we are suffering the consequences of what we did to our brother; we saw the great trouble he was in when he begged for help, but we would not listen.

That is why we are in this trouble now." Reuben said, I told you not to harm the boy, but you will not listen. And now we are being paid back for his death." Joseph understood what they said, but they did not know it, because they have been speaking to him through an interpreter. Joseph left them and began to cry. When he was able to speak again, he came back picked out Simeon, and had him tied up in front of them. **Joseph brothers returned to Canaan:** Joseph gave orders to fill his brother's packs with grain, to put each man's money back in his sack, and to give them food for the trip. This was done. The brothers loaded their donkeys with grain they had bought, and then they left. At the place where they spent the night, one of them opened the sack to feed the donkey and found the money at the top of the sack. My money had been returned to me, he called to his brothers. "Here it is in my sack. Their hearts sank, and in fear they ask one another, "What has God done to us?" When they came to their father Jacob in Canaan, they told him all that had happened to them; the governor of Egypt spoke harshly to us and accused us of spying against his country. We are not spies we answered, we are honest men. We were twelve brothers in all, sons of the same father. One brother is dead, and the youngest is still in Canaan with our father. The man answered, "This is how I will find out if you are honest men; one of you will stay with me; the rest will take grain for your starving families and leave. Bring your youngest brother to me. Then I will know you are not spies, but honest men:

I will give your brother back to you, and you can stay here and trade. Then when they emptied out their sacks, every one of them found his bag of money, they and their father Jacob were afraid. Their father said to them, "Do you want me to lose all my children? Joseph is gone; Simeon is gone; and now you want to take away Benjamin. I am the one who suffers. Reuben said to his father, "If I don't bring Benjamin back to you, you can kill my two sons. "Put him in my care and I will bring him back." But Jacob said, "My son cannot go with you; his brother is dead, and he is the only one left. Something might happen to him on the way, I am an old man, and the sorrow you will cause me will kill me."

Joseph brothers returned to Egypt with Benjamin; The famine in Canaan got worse, and when the family of Jacob had eaten all the grain which had been brought from Egypt, Jacob said to his sons, "Go back and buy a little food for us." Judah said to him, "The man sternly warned us that we would not be admitted into his presence unless we had our brother with us. If you are willing to send our brother with us we will go and buy food for you. If you are not willing, we will not go, because the man told us that we would not be admitted into his presence unless our brother was with us. Jacob said why you have caused me so much trouble by telling the man that

you had another brother? They answered, "The man kept asking about us and our family, Is your father still living? Do you
have another brother?

We had to answer his questions. How could we know that
he would tell us to bring our brother with us? Judah said to
his father send the boy with me, and we will leave at once.
Then none of us will starve to death. I will pledge my own life,
and you can hold me responsible for him. If I don't bring him
back to you safe and sound, I will always bear the blame. "If
we had not waited so long, we could have been there, and
back twice by now." Their father said; if that is how it has to
be, then take the best products of the land in your packs as a
present for the governor; a little resin, a little honey, spices,
pistachio nuts, and almonds. And take with you also as much
money because you must take back the money that was returned in the top of your sacks. Maybe it was a mistake. Take
your brother and return at once.

May Almighty God cause the man to have pity on you, so
that he will give Benjamin and your other brother back to
you: As for me, if I must lose my children I must lose them:
So, the brothers took the gifts and as much money, and set
out for Egypt with Benjamin. There they presented themselves
to Joseph. When Joseph saw Benjamin with them, he said to
the servants in charge of the house: Take these men to my
house. They are going to eat with me at noon, so kill an animal and prepare it. The servants did as he was commanded
and took the brothers to Joseph's house. As they were being
brought to the house, they were afraid, and thought, "We are
being brought here because of the money that was returned
in our sacks the first time. They will suddenly attack us, take

our donkeys, and make us his slaves." So, at the door of the house, they said to the servants in charge, if you please, sir, we came here once before to buy food. When we set up camp on our way home, we opened our sacks, and each man found his money in the top of his sack—every pit of it. We have brought it back to you. We have also brought some more money with us to buy more food. We do not know who put our money back in our sacks. The servants said, "Don't worry. Don't be afraid. Your God, The God of your forefather, must have put the money in your sacks for you. I received your payment. Then he brought Simeon to them. The servants took the brothers into the house, He gave them water so that they could wash their feet, and he fed their donkeys. They got their gift ready to present to Joseph when he arrived at noon, because they had been told that they were to eat with him. When Joseph got home, they took their gifts into the house to him and bowed down to the ground before him. He asked about their health and then said, you told me about your old father—how is he? He is still alive and well." And they knelt and bowed down before him. When Joseph saw his brother Benjamin, he said, so this is your youngest brother, the one you told me about. God bless you, my son. "Then Joseph left suddenly, because his heart was full of tender feelings for his brother.

He was about to break down, so he went to his room and cried. After he had washed his face, he came out, and controlling himself, he ordered the meal to be served. Joseph was served at one table and his brothers at another table: the Egyptian's who were eating there were served separately, because they considered it beneath their dignity to eat with Hebrews. The brothers had seated at the table, facing Joseph, in the order of their age from the oldest to the youngest. When they saw how they had been seated, they looked at one another in amazement. Food was served to them from Joseph's table, and Benjamin was served as five times as much as the rest of them. So, they ate and drank with Joseph until they were drunk. **The missing cup:** Genesis chapter 44; Joseph commanded the servant in charge of the house, "Fill the men's sack with as much food as they can carry, and put each man's money in the top of his sack. Put my silver cup in the top of the youngest brother's sack, together with his money in the grain. "He did as he was told. Early in the morning the brothers were sent on their way with their donkeys. When they had gone only a short distance from the city, Joseph said to the servant in charge of his house, "Hurry after those men. When you catch up with them, ask them, why have you paid back evil for good? Why did you steal my master's silver cup? It is the one he drinks from, the one he uses for divination.

You have committed a serious crime. When the servants caught up with them he repeated the same words. They answered him, "What do you mean, sir, by talking like this? We swear that we have done no such thing. You know that we brought back to you from the land of Canaan the money we found in the top of our sacks. Why then should we steal silver or gold from your master's house? Sir, if any of is found to have it, he should be put to death, and the rest of us would become your salves." He said, I agree; but only the one who has the taken the cup will be my slave, and the rest of you can go free. So, they quickly lowered their sacks to the ground, and each man opened his sack. Joseph's servants search carefully, beginning with the oldest and ending with the youngest, and the cup was found in Benjamin's sack. The brothers torn their clothes in sorrow, loaded their donkeys, and returned to the city. When Judah and his brothers came to Joseph's house, he was still there. They bowed down before him, and Joseph said, "What you have done? Didn't you know that a man in my position could find you out by practicing divination? What can we say to you sir? Judah answered. "How can we argue? How can we clear ourselves? God has uncovered our guilt. All of us are now your slaves and not just the one with whom the cup was found." Joseph said, "Oh no; I would never do that. Only the one who had the cup would be my slave. The rest of you may go back to your father safe and sound.

Judah pleads for Benjamin; Judah went up to Joseph and said, "Please sir, allow me to speak with you freely. Don't be angry with me; you are like the king himself. Sir, you asked us, do you have a father or another brother? We answered; we have a father who is old and a younger brother, born to him in his old age. The boy's brother is dead, and is the only one of his mother's children still alive; his father loves him very much. Sir, you told us to bring him here, so that you could see him, and we answered that the boy could not leave his father; if he did, his father would do. Then you said, you will not be admitted into your presence again unless your youngest brother comes with you." When we went back to our father, we told him what you have said. Then he told us to return to buy a little food. We answered, we cannot **go**; we will not be admitted into the man's presence again unless our youngest brother is with us. We can go only if our youngest brother goes also. Our father said to us, "You know that my wife Rachael bore me only two sons. One of them had already left me. He must have been torn to pieces by wild animals, because I have not seen him since he left. If you take this one from me now and something happens to him, the sorrow you would cause me would kill me, as old as I am. And now, sir, Judah continued,

"If I go back to my father without the boy, as soon as he sees that the boy is not with me, he will die. His life is wrapped up with the life of the boy, and he is so old that the sorrow we will cause him will kill him. What is more, I pledged my life to my father for the boy. I told him that if I did not bring the boy back to him, I would bear the blame all my life. And now, sir, I will stay here as your slave in place of the boy; Let him go back with his brothers. How can I go back to my father if the boy is not with me? I cannot bear to see this disaster come upon my father." **Joseph told his brothers who he is.** Joseph was no longer able to control his feelings in front of his servants, so he ordered them all to leave the room. No one else was with him when Joseph told his brothers who he was. He cried with such loud sobs that the Egyptians heard of it, and the news was taken to the king's palace. Joseph said to his brothers, "I am Joseph. Is my father still alive? But when the brothers heard this, they were so terrified that they could not answer. Then Joseph said to them, please come closer." They did, and he said to them, "I am your brother Joseph, whom you sold into Egypt. Now do not be upset or blame yourselves because you sold me here. It was really God who sent me ahead of you to save people's lives. This is only the second year of famine in the land; there will be five more years in which there will be neither plowing nor reaping. God sent me ahead of you to rescue you in this amazing way and to make sure that you and your descendants survive.

So, it was not really you who sent me here, but God. He has made me the king highest official. I am in charge of his whole country; I am the ruler of Egypt. "Now hurry back to my father and tell him that this is what his son Joseph says; God has made me ruler of all Egypt; come to me without delay. You can live in the region of Goshen, where you can be near me—you, your children, your grandchildren, your sheep, your goats, your cattle, and everything else that you have. If you are in Goshen, I can take care of you. There will still be five years of famine; and I do not want you, your family, and your livestock to starve. "Joseph continued, now all of you, and you too, Benjamin, can see that I am really Joseph. Tell my father how powerful I am here in Egypt and tell him about everything that you have seen. Then hurry and bring him here. He threw is arms around his brother Benjamin and began to cry; Benjamin also cried as he hugged him. Then, still weeping, he embraced each of his brothers and kissed them. After that his brothers began to talk with him. When the news reached the palace that Joseph's brothers had come, the king and the officials were pleased. He said to Joseph, "Tell your brothers to load their animals and to return to the land of Canaan. Let them get their father and their families to come back here. I will give them the best land in Egypt, and they will have more than enough to live on.

Tell them also to take wagons with them from Egypt for their wives and small children and to bring their father with them. They are not to worry about leaving their possessions behind; the best in the whole land of Egypt will be theirs." Jacob's sons did as they were told and Joseph gave everyone wagons as the king had ordered, and food for the trip. He also gave each of them a change of clothes, but he gave Benjamin three hundred pieces of silver and five changes of clothes. He sent his father five donkeys loaded with the best Egyptian goods and ten donkeys loaded with grain, bread, and other food for the trip. He sent his brothers off as they left, he said to them, **"Don't quarrel on the way."** They left Egypt and went back home to their father Jacob in Canaan. "Joseph is still alive." they told him. "He is the ruler of all Egypt. "Jacob was stunned and could not believe them. But when they told him all that Joseph had said to them, and when he saw the wagons which Joseph had sent to take him to Egypt, he recovered from the shock. "My son Joseph is still alive, he said. This is all that I could ask for. I must go and see him before I die. Jacob and his family go to Egypt. Jacob packed up all he had and went to Beersheba, where he offered sacrifices to the God of his father Isaac. God spoke to him in a vision at night and called, Jacob, Jacob. "Yes here I am, he answered. I am God, the God of your father, he said. Do not be afraid to go to Egypt; I will make your descendants great nations there.

I will go with you to Egypt, and I will bring your descendants back to this land. Joseph will be with you when you die." Jacob set out from Beersheba. His sons put him, their small children, and their wives in the wagons which the king of Egypt had sent. They took their livestock and the possession they had acquired in Canaan and went to Egypt. Jacob took all his descendants with him: his sons, his grandsons, his daughters, and his granddaughters. **Jacob and his family in Egypt:** Jacob sent Judah ahead to ask Joseph to meet with him in Goshen. When they arrived, Joseph got in his chariot and went to Goshen to meet his father. When they met, Joseph threw his arms around his father's neck and cried for a long time. Jacob said to Joseph, "I am ready to die, now that I have seen you and know that you are still alive." Then Joseph said to his brothers and the rest of his father's family, "I must go and tell the king that my brothers and all my father's family, who were living in Canaan, have come to me. I will tell him that you are shepherds and take care of livestock and that you have brought your flocks and herds and everything that belongs to you. When the king calls for you and asks what your occupation is, be sure to tell him that you have been taken care of livestock all your lives, just as your ancestors did. In this way he will let you live the region of Goshen. "Joseph said this because Egyptians will have nothing to do with shepherds. So Joseph took five of his brothers and went to the king.

He told him, "My father and my brothers have come from Canaan with their flocks, their herds, and all that they own. They are now in the region of Goshen. He then presented his brothers to the king. The king asked them, "What is your occupation. "We are shepherd, sir, just as our ancestors were, they answered. "We have come to live in this country, because in the land of Canaan the famine is so severe that there is no pasture for our flocks. Please give us permission to live in the region of Goshen. The king said to Joseph, now that your father and your brothers have arrived, the land of Egypt is theirs. Let them settle in the region of Goshen, the best part of the land. And if there are capable men among them, put them in charge of my own livestock. Then Joseph brought his father Jacob and presented him to the king. Jacob gave the king his blessing, and the king asked him, how old are you? **Jacob answered, "My life of wandering has lasted a hundred and thirty years. Those years had been few and difficult, unlike the long years of my ancestors in their wanderings**." Jacob gave the king a farewell blessing and left. Then Joseph settled his father and his brothers in Egypt, giving them property in the best of the land near the city of Ramesses, as the king had commanded. Joseph provided food for his father, his brothers, and all the rest of his family, including the very youngest. **THE**

FAMINE: The famine was so severe that there was no food anywhere, and the people of Egypt and Canaan became very weak with hunger. As they bought grain Joseph collected all the money and took it to the palace. When all the money in Egypt and in Canaan was spent, the Egyptians came to Joseph and said, "Give us food; don't let us die. Do something our money is all gone. So, they brought their livestock to Joseph, and he gave them food for exchange for their horses, sheep, goats, cattle, and donkeys. That year he supplied them with food in exchange for all their livestock. The following year they came to him and said, "We will not hide the fact from you, sir, that our money is all gone, and all our livestock belongs to you. There is nothing else to give to you except our bodies and our land. Don't let us die. Do something; "Don't let our fields to be deserted. Buy us and our land in exchange for food. We all will be the king's slaves, and he will own our land. Give us grain to keep us alive and seed so that we can plant our fields. Joseph bought all the land of Egypt for the king. Every Egyptians was forced to sell their land, because the famine was so severe; and all the lands became the king's property. Joseph made slaves of the people from one end of Egypt to the other. The only land that he did not buy was the land that belongs to the priests. They did not have to sell their lands, because the king gave them allowance to live on. So, Joseph said, to the people, you see, I have now bought you and your lands for the king.

Here is the seed for you to sow in your fields. At the time of harvest, you must give one-fifth to the king. You can use the

rest for seed and for food for yourselves and for your families."
They answered, "You have saved our lives; you have been
good to us, sir, and we will be the king's slaves. So Joseph
made it a law for the land of Egypt that one-fifth of the harvest should belong to the king. This law still remains in force
today. Only the land of the priests did not become the king's
property. Jacob last request; The Israelites lived in Egypt in the
region of Goshen, where they became rich, and have many
children. Jacob lived in Egypt seventeen years, until he was
a hundred and forty-seven years old. When the time draws
near for him to die, he called for his son Joseph and said
to him, "Place your hands between my thighs and make a
solemn vow that you will not bury me in Egypt. I want to
be buried were my fathers are; carry me out of Egypt and
bury me, where they are buried." Joseph said, I will do as you
say." Jacob said make a vow that you will. Joseph made the
vow, and Jacob gave thanks there on his bed. Sometime later
Joseph was told that his father was ill. So he took his two sons,
Manasseh and Ephraim, and went to see Jacob. When Jacob
was told that his son Joseph had come to see him, he gathered
his strength and sat up in bed. Jacob said to Joseph, Almighty
God appeared to me at Luz in the land of Canaan and blessed
me. He said to me, I will give you many children, so that your
descendants will become many nations; I will give this land
for your descendants as their possession forever.

When Jacob finished giving instructions to his sons, he laid
back down and died. Joseph threw himself on his father, crying and kissing his face. Then Joseph gave orders to embalm
his father's body. It took forty days the normal time for em-
balming. The Egyptians mourned for him for seventy days.
When the time of mourning was over, Joseph said to the king

officials, please take this message to the king. When my father was about to die, he made me promise, that I would bury him in the tomb which he had prepared in the land of Canaan. So please let me go and bury my father, and then I will come back. The answered, "Go bury your father, as you promised you would. So Joseph went to bury his father, All the king's officials, the senior men of his court, and all the leading men of Egypt went with Joseph. His family, his brothers, and the rest of his father's family all went with him. Only their small children, their sheep and goats, and cattle stayed in the region of Goshen. Men in chariots and men on horseback also went with him; it was a huge group. When they came to the threshing place at Atad, east of the Jordan, they mourned loudly for a long time, and Joseph performed mourning ceremonies for seven days. When the citizens of Canaan saw those people mourning at Atad, they said, "What a solemn ceremony the Egyptians are holding. That is why the place is called Abel Miriam.

So Jacob's sons did as he had commanded them. ; They carried his body and buried him in the cave at Machpelah east of Mamre in the field which Abraham had bought from Ephron the Hittites for a burial ground. After Joseph had buried his father, he returned to Egypt with his brothers and all who had gone with him for the funeral. **Joseph reassures his brothers.** After the death of their father Jacob; Joseph brothers said, "What if Joseph still hates us and plans to pay us back for all the harm we did to him? So they sent a massager to Joseph: Before our father died, he told us to ask you, "Please forgive the crime your brothers committed when they wronged you, now please forgive us the wrong that we, the servants of your father's God, have done.

Joseph cried when he received this message. Then his brothers came themselves and bowed down before him. "Here we are before you, as your slaves, they said. But Joseph said to them, "Don't be afraid; I can't put myself in the place of God. You plotted evil against me, but God turn it into good, in order to preserve the lives of many people who are alive today because of what happened. You have nothing to fear. I will take care of you and your children." So he reassured them with kind words that touched their hearts. **Genesis Chapter 40**

CHAPTER 15

The Final Battle is Won by Faith and Courage

2 King chapter 17-20

Elijah and the drought; A prophet named Elijah, from Tishbe in Gilead, said to king Ahab, "In the name of the Lord, the living God of Israel, whomI serve, I tell you that there will be no dew or rain for the next two or three years until I say so." Then the Lord sad to Elijah, leave this place and go east and hide yourself near the Cherith Brook, east of Jordan. The brook will supply you with water to drink, and I have commanded ravens to bring you food there." Elijah obeyed the Lord's command, and went and stayed by Cherith Brook. He drank water from the Brook, and ravens brought him bread and meat every morning and every evening.

After a while the brook dried up because of lack of rain. **Elijah and the Widow in Zarephath:** Then the Lord said to Elijah, Now go to the town of Zarephath, near Sidon, and stay there. I have commanded a widow who lives there to feed you. So Ejilah went to Zarephath, and as he came to the town gate, he saw widow gathering firewood. "Please bring me a drink of water, he said to her. As she was going to get it, he called out, "And please brings me some bread, too. She answered, "By the living Lord your God I swear that I don't have any bread. All I have is a handful of flours in a bowl and a bit of olive oil in a jar. I came here to gather some firewood to take back home and prepare what a little I have for my son and me. That will be the last meal, and then we will starve to death. Doesn't worry, Elisha say to her? "Go on and prepare your meal. But first make a small loaf from what you have and bring it to me, and then prepare the rest for you and your son. For this is what the Lord, the God of Israel says; "The bowl will not run out of flour or the jar run out of oil before the days that, I the Lord, send rain. The widow went and did as Elijah had told her; and all of them had enough food for many days. As the Lord had promised through Elijah, the bowl did not run out of flour, nor did the jar run out of oil.

Elijah and the prophets of Baal: After sometime, in the third year of the drought, the Lord said to Elijah, "Go and present yourself to king Ahab, and I will send you rain." So, Elijah started out. The famine in Samaria was at his worst, so Ahab called in Obadiah, who was in charge of the palace. Obadiah was a devote worshipper of the Lord, and when Jezebel was killing the Lord's prophets, Obadiah took a hundred of them, hid them with food and water. Ahab said to Obadiah, "Let us go and look at every spring and every stream bed in the land to see if we can find enough grass to keep the horses and mules alive. Maybe we won't have to kill any of our animals. They agreed on which part of the land each one would explore, and set off in different directions. As Obadiah was on his way, he suddenly met Elijah. He recognized him, bowed low before him, and asked, "Is it really you sir?" Yes, I am Elijah he answered. "Go and tell your master the king that I am here." Obadiah answered, "What have I done that you want to put me in danger of being killed by the king Ahab? By the living Lord, your God, I swear that the king has made a search for you in every country in the world. Whenever the ruler of a country reported that you were not in his country, Ahab would require that ruler to swear that you could not be found. And now you want me to go and tell him that you are here? What if the spirit of the Lord carries you off to some unknown place as soon as I leave? Then, when I tell Ahab that you are her and he can't find you, he will put me to death. Remember that I have been a devout worshipper of the Lord ever since I was a boy. Haven't you heard that? When Jezebel was killing the Prophets of the Lord I hid a hundreds of them in caves, in two groups of fifty, and supplied them with food and water? So how can you order me to go and tell the king you are here? He will kill me. Elijah answered, by the living Lord Almighty, whom I serve; I promise that I will present myself to the king today. So Obadiah went to the king Ahab and told him, and Ahab set off to meet Elijah. When Ahab saw him, he said, "So there you are—the worst trouble maker in Israel. I am not the trouble maker, "Elijah answered. You are— you and your father. You are disobeying the Lord commands and worshipping the idols of Baal. Now order all the people of Israel to meet me at Mount Carmel. Bring along the 450 prophets of Baal and the 400 prophets of the goddess Asherah who are supported by Queen Jezebel. So Ahab summoned all the Israelites and the prophets of Baal to meet at Mount Carmel. Elijah went up to the people and said, "How much longer will it take you to make your minds? If the Lord is God, worship him. But if Baal is God, worship him; but the people did not say a word. Then Elijah said, "I am the only prophets of the Lord who is still left, but there are 450 prophets of Baal. Bring two bulls; let the prophets of Baal take one, kill it, cut it in pieces, and put it on the wood—but don't light the fire. I will do the same with the other bull. Then lets the prophets of Baal pray to their god, and I will pray to the Lord, and the one who answered by sending fire—he is God. The people shouted their approval.

Then Elijah said to the prophets of Baal, "Since there are many of you, you take a bull and prepare it first. Pray to your god, but don't set fire to the wood. They took the bull that was brought to them, prepare it, and prayed to Baal until noon. They shouted answer us, Baal; and kept dancing around the altar they had built. But no answer came. At noon Elijah started making fun of them; "Pray louder; he is god; maybe he is day-dreaming or relieving himself, or perhaps he gone off on a trip. Or maybe he is sleeping, and you have got to wake him up. So the prophets of Baal prayed louder, and cut themselves with knives and daggers, according to their ritual, until blood flowed. They kept on ranting and raving until the middle of the afternoon; but no answer came, not a sound was heard. Then Elijah said to the people, "Come closer to me. "And they all gathered around him. He set about repairing the altar of the Lord which had been torn down. He took twelves stones, one of each of the twelve tribes, named for the sons of Jacob, the man by whom the Lord had given the name Israel. With these stones he rebuilt the altar for the worship of the Lord. He dug a trench around it, large enough to hold about four gallons of water. Then he placed the wood upon the altar; cut the bull in pieces, and laid it on the wood. He said, "Fill four jars with water and pour it on the offering and the wood."

They did so, and he said, Do it again"—and they did. Do it one more time and they did:

The water ran down around the altar and filled the trench. At the hour of the afternoon sacrifice the Prophets Elijah approached the altar and prayed. "OH Lord, the God of Abraham, Isaac, and Jacob, prove now that you the God of Israel and I am your servant and I have done all this at your command. Answer me, Lord; answer me, so that this people will know that you, the Lord, are God and that you are bringing them back to yourself." The Lord sent fire down, and it burned up the sacrifice, the wood, and the stones, scorched the earth and dried up the water in the trench. When the people saw this, they threw themselves on the ground and exclaimed, "The Lord is God; The Lord alone is God. Elijah ordered, seize all the prophets of Baal; don't let any of them get away. The people seized them all, and Elijah led them down to Kishon Brook and killed them. **The end of the drought:** Then Elijah said to king Ahab, "Now go and eat. I hear the roaring rain approaching. While Ahab went to eat, Elijah climbed to the top of Mount Carmel, where he bowed down to the ground, with his head between his knees. He said to his servants "Go and look towards the sea. "The servants went and returned saying, "I didn't see a thing. "Seven times in all Elijah told him to go and look. The seventh times he returned and said, "I saw a little cloud no bigger than a man's hand, coming up from the sea. Elijah ordered his servant, "Go to king Ahab and tell him to get in his chariot and go back home before the rains stop him. In a little while the sky was covered with dark clouds, the wind began to blow; and a heavy rain began to fall.

Ahab got in his chariot and started back to Jezreel. The power of the Lord came upon Elijah; he fastened his clothes tight around his waist and ran ahead of Ahab all the way to Jezreel. Elijah on mount Sanai. 1 King chapter 19 verses 1—21; King Ahab told his wife Jezebel everything that Elijah had done and how he had put all the prophets of Baal to death. She sent a message to Elijah; "May the gods strike me dead if by this time tomorrow I don't do the same thing to you that you did to the prophets. Elijah was afraid and fled for his life; he took his servant and went to Beersheba in Judah. Leaving his servants there, Elijah walked a whole day into the wilderness. He stopped and sat down in the shade of a tree, and wished he would die, "It is too much, Lord, "he prayed. "Take away my life; I might as well be dead." He lies down under the tree and fell asleep. Suddenly an Angel touched him and said, "Wake up and eat. He looked around and saw a loaf of bread and a jar of water near his head. He ate and drank and lay down again. This happened twice. Elijah got up, ate and drank, and the food gave him enough strength to walk forty days to Sanai, the holy mountain. There he went to into a cave to spend the night. When the Lord was passing by, Elijah looked. But the Lord was not in the wind, (Hurricane). And the Lord was not in the earth quake either, nor in the fire but in a small still voice .

The final battle and victory: Roman 9:15-16: For he says to Moses, **"I will have mercy on whomever I will have mercy, and I will have compassion on whomever I will have compassion**. So it is not of him, who wills, nor of him who runs, but of God who shows mercy. Roman 8:35-39; who shall separate us from the love of Christ? Shall tribulation, or distress, or persecution, or famine, or nakedness, or peril, or sword? Yet in all these things we are more than conquerors through him who loved us. For I am persuaded that neither death nor life, nor angels nor principalities nor powers, nor things present, nor things to come, nor height nor depth, nor any other created thing, shall be able to separate us from the love of God, which is in Christ Jesus our Lord.

None of the rulers of this world knew this wisdom. If they had known it, they would not have crucified the Lord of Glory. 1 Corinthians Chapter 2 verses 8: And Revelation 12:11; they overcame him by the blood of the lamb, and by the word of their testimony, and they were will to give up their lives and die. Revelation 20:8-9, Satan brought them all together for battle. But fire came down from heaven and destroyed them. Revelation 21:8, But cowards, traitors, perverts, murderers, the immoral, those who practice magic, those who worship idols, and all liars—the place for them is the lake burning with fire and sulfur.

CHAPTER 16

The Battle of Armageddon

The word "Armageddon comes from a Hebrew word Har-Magedo, "Mount Megiddo" and has been synonymous with the future battle in which God will intervene and destroy the armies of the Antichrist as predicted in biblical prophecy (Revelation 16verses 16; and Revelation 20 verses1-10). This frightening apocalyptic word "Armageddon" refers to earth's final battle which is generally referred to as the Battle of Armageddon. But who are the contestants of this great battle of Armageddon? A fairly common reply would be "Russia, Syria, or Iran against Israel." As the Middle East simmers toward a boiling point, and as US, British, and Israeli intelligence monitor closely Iran's quest for a nuclear bomb which might even be used against America. Millions of Christians, Jews, Muslims, and even secularists are pondering, "Is the battle of

Armageddon at hand?" I believe so. Yet nobody knows when. Take a look for yourself the verses and the chapter of the book of Revelation chapter 16 verses 12-21. Christ as the righteous warrior, for we see him coming battle with the host of Satan's armies in what is often called "the Armageddon, "but which in truth is a war, or campaign, of the great day of God Almighty. This war necessitated by the fiendishly evil ambitions of humankind and the evil source of power, Satan. Our Lord himself tells when this battle will take place; "Immediately after the distress of those days "the sun will be darkened, and the moon will not its light; the stars will fall from sky, and the heavenly bodies will be shaken. At that time the sign of the son of man will appear in the sky, and all the nations of the earth will mourn. They will see the son of man coming on the cloud of the sky, with power and great glory. And he will send his angels with a loud trumpet call, and they will gather his elect from the four winds, from one end of the heavens to the other. The glorious appearance will take place, immediately after the distress of those days, that is, at the end of the tribulation and before the millennium.

Our Lord will time his coming at the most dramatic point in all history. The Antichrist, the false prophet, and Satan will inspire the armies of the world to invade Palestine in a gigantic effort to rid the world of the Jews and to fight against Christ. This coming battle before Christ sets up his millennial kingdom is often called "the Battle of Armageddon. This misleading expression because Armageddon means "Mount of Slaughter" and refers to the beautiful valley to the east of Mount Megiddo, and the word battle" here literally means "campaign" or "war". No war has ever been won by a single battle. In fact, it is possible to lose a battle and still win a war. The war of the great day of God almighty takes place in a single day, and the Battle of Armageddon will be just one of the battles of that war.

CHAPTER 17

The Apocalyptic War Foretold by the Bible

Current predictions about the future of the world run from the utopian to the cataclysmic. Is the world headed for a bright or dismal future, or both? Will humanity overcome its legacy of centuries of conflict and short sighted exploitation and build a unified society of peace and harmony? Or will the earth descend into chaos and become an environmental waste-land? The prophets of the Bible foretold amazing things about the future. Many of their predictions have already come to pass. For instance, there are over 400 prophecies about Jesus Christ, all written down hundreds of years before his birth , that were fulfilled during his lifetime on earth.

The chance of even eight of those prophecies being fulfilled in one man have been calculated at one chance in one hundred million billion. More importantly for us now, there are hundreds more biblical prophecies about future events and world conditions. Some of these are now being fulfilled in our times, and they presage the fulfillment of yet others in the near future, even in our lifetimes. These future events are of such size and scope, and are so momentous in nature, that you will want to be prepared for them when they happen. Our future was predicted thousands of years ago. You can know that future. The following is a short summary of the events and conditions the Bible predicts are to come in chorological order. **Signs of the times:** Today, conditions prevail and events are taking place that Jesus said would signal his return and the end of the world as we know it. Jesus, as well as several biblical writers, likened these signs to a woman in labor prior to giving birth. Many of these "birth pains" such as war, famine, earthquakes, and pestilences, have been evident for a long time. Yet man has in this modern age invented weapons capable of previously unheard of death and mass destruction. Famine is a reality for millions, and the UN Food and Agriculture Organization estimates that 800 million people go hungry each day, and malnutrition in children contributes to over half of child deaths: Pollution, global warming, and the depletion of resources points toward even greater famine and resultant violence in the near future.

And the Gospel has been taught in all nations like never before in the course of history, by radio, television, and internet. As Jesus was sitting in the Mount of Olives, the disciples came to him privately. Tell us they said, "What will be the sign of your coming and of the end of this age? Jesus answered. You will hear of wars and rumors of wars, but see to it that you are not alarmed. Such things must happen, but the end is still to come. Nation will rise against nation, and kingdom against kingdom. There will be famines and earthquakes in various places. All these are the beginning of birth pains. "Because of the increase of wickedness, the love of most will grow cold, but he who stands firm to the end will be saved. And this Gospel of the kingdom will be preached in the whole world as a testimony to all nations and then the end will come: "Matthew chapter 24 verses 3-14). "But Daniel, keep this prophecy a secret; seal it up so that it will not be understood until the end times, when travel and education shall be vastly increased. Daniel Chapter 12 verses 2-4) **The Antichrist;** An evil man—called many things by the prophets, but most commonly referred to today as the "Antichrist"—will come to power at the head of a world government.

His evil nature will at first not be so evident, and many will regard as a savior because he will be able to bring solutions to some of the world's most intractable problems such as a more equitable distribution and consumption of resources; resolution of long-standing hostilities between nations, ideologies, and religions; and reduction of economic instability and exploitation. He will be a man of war and yet gain power by both intrigue and nonbelligerent means. He is, however, in league with Satan, and in the end, will become the embodiment of evil. It is the last hour; as you have heard that the Antichrist is coming. (1 John Chapter 2 verses18) Let no one deceive you by any means; for that Day will not come unless the falling away comes first, and the man of sin is revealed, the son of perdition, who oppose and exalts himself above all that is called God or that is worshipped, so that he sits as God in the temple of God, showing himself that he is God. The coming of the lawless one is according to the working of Satan, with all power, signs, and lying wonders: (2 Thessalonians Chapter 2 verses 3-9). This vile person--- shall come in peaceably, and seize the kingdom by intrigue--He shall do what his fathers have not done, nor his forefathers: he shall disperse among them plunder, spoil, and riches; and he shall devise his plans against the strongholds, but only for a time. (Daniel Chapter 11 verses 21-25). When the transgressors have reached their fullness, {this} king shall arise, having fierce features, who understands sinister schemes. His power shall be mighty, but not by his own power; he shall destroy fearfully, and shall prosper and thrive; and also the holy people.

He shall destroy the mighty, and also the holy people. Through his cunning he shall cause deceit to prosper under his rule; and he shall exalt himself in his heart. He shall destroy many in their prosperity. He shall even rise against the Price of princes; but he shall be broken without human means; (Daniel Chapter 8 verses 23-25). So they worshipped (Satan) who gave authority to the beast {Antichrist}; and they worshipped the beast, saying "Who is like the beast?" And authority was given him over every tribe, tongue, and nation. All who dwell on the earth will worship him, whose names have not been written in the Book of Life (Revelation chapter 13 verses 4-8). **The Covenant:** The Antichrist will initiate, or at the least be very much involved in, an agreement called in the Bible the "Holy Covenant," that temporarily brings a measure of peace and security to the world. It will include a solution to the vexing problem of just Israel/Palestinian settlement. This agreement will allow the rebuilding of the Jewish Temple in Jerusalem. The signing of this covenant will signal the start of the last seven years of man's dominion on Earth. Approximately three and a half years into the agreement, after surviving what may likely be an assassination attempt, the megalomaniacal Antichrist will break the covenant, declare himself God, and abolish all religious worship except that of himself.

He will confirm a covenant with many for one "seven" (seven years) he will put an end to sacrifice and offering (religious rites). And after the league is made with (the Antichrist) shall act deceitfully, for he shall come up and become strong with a small number of people--- his heart shall be moved against the holy covenant; so he shall – rage against the holy covenant, and do damage—Those who do wickedly against the covenant he shall corrupt with flattery. (Daniel Chapter 11 verses 23-32). Then I stood on the sand of the sea. And I saw a beast rising up out of the sea, having seven heads.....And I saw one of his heads {the Antichrist} as if it had been mortally wounded, and his deadly wound was healed. And the entire world marveled and followed the beast. (Revelation Chapter 13 verses 1-3).

The Image of the Beast: When the Antichrist breaks the covenant; the mysterious Abomination of Desolation is erected in the precincts of the Jewish Temple. The prophet Daniel wrote of it a number of times, and Jesus confirmed that when it is put in its place it will signal the beginning of the 1260-day period known as the great tribulation. Daniel refers several times to this Abomination's capacity to bring desolation. In the book of Revelation is called the image of the Beast, and it has power to cause those that do not worship it to be killed. It could be some sort of cybernetic representation of the Antichrist endowed with artificial intelligence allowing it to speak and issue orders. The Antichrist's government demands its worship: However, those who willingly comply are condemned to the same fate awaiting the diabolical Antichrist.

And forces shall be mustered by the Antichrist, and they shall defile the sanctuary fortress; then they shall take away the daily sacrifices, and place there the abomination of desolation. (Daniel Chapter 11 verses 31). Therefore, when you see the "abomination of desolation," spoken of by Daniel the prophet, standing in the holy place.... then there will be great tribulation, such as has not been since the beginning of the world until this time, no, nor ever shall be. (Matthew Chapter 24 verses 15-21). {The Antichrist's False Prophet} deceives those who dwell on the earth by those signs which he was granted to do in the sight of the beast, telling those who dwell on the earth to make an image to the beast who was wounded by the sword and lived. He was granted power to give breath to the image of the beast, that the image of the beast should both speak and cause as many as would not worship the image of the beast to be killed.(Revelation Chapter 13 verses14-16) {An angel said} with a loud voice, "If anyone worships the beast and his image, and received the mark on his forehead or on his hand, he himself shall drink of the wine of the wrath of God, which is poured out full strength into the cup of his indignation, He shall be tormented with fire and brimstone in the presence of the holy angels and in the presence of the Lamb (Revelation Chapter 14 verses 9-10). Also see Daniel Chapter 9 verses 27:

The Great Tribulation: After the covenant is broken, the next three and a half years will see the world plunge into unprecedented social chaos. This period of time is known as the "Great Tribulation". The Antichrist becomes fully possessed by Satan, and his government will persecute those who refuse to worship him. An electronic monetary system will be put in place, and everyone wishing to "buy and sell" will be required to receive the "mark of the Beast." This will be personalized account number somehow embedded, probably in the form of an electronic chip, in people's right hand or foreheads. This account number is enigmatically linked to the number 666. God's word warns people not to receive this mark. Meanwhile, God helps those Christians and others, who resist the Antichrist, and in their defense, unleashes horrific pestilences and plagues on the Antichrist and his followers. We are also told how two of God's End time prophets will perform miracles and publicly defy the Antichrist. These two are probably not alone in having these powers available to them, as other believers could have comparable abilities. For then there will be great distress, unequaled from the beginning of the world until now- and never to be equaled again. If those days had not been cut short, no one would survive, but for the sake of the elect those days will be shortened.

Matthew Chapter 24 verses21-23): He causes all, both small and great, rich and poor, free and slave, to receive a mark on their right hand or on their foreheads, and that no one will buy or sell except one who has the mark or the name of the beast, or the number of his name. Here is wisdom. Let him who has understanding calculate the number of the beast, for it is the number of a man: His number is 666. (Revelation chapter 13 verses16-18): The woman (symbolizing the believers in Jesus) was given two wings of great eagle, that she might fly into the wilderness to her place, where she is nourished for a time and times and half a time, from the presence of the serpent.... And the dragon was enraged with the woman, and he went to make war with the rest of her offspring, who keep the commandments of God and have the testimony of Jesus Christ.(Revelation chapter 12 verses14-17)But the people who know their God shall be strong, and carry out great exploits. Then out of the smoke locusts came upon the earth. And to them was given power, as the scorpions of the earth have power. They were committed not to harm the grass of the earth, or any green thing, or any tree, but only those men who do not have the seal of God on their foreheads. And they were given authority to kill them, but to torment them for five months. And their torment was like the torment of a scorpion when it strikes a man. In those days men will seek death and will not find it; they will desire to die, and death will flee from them. (Revelation chapter 9 verses 3-6). (An angel) will give power to two witnesses, and they will prophesy one thousand two hundred and sixty days, clothed in sackcloth---

And if anyone wants to harm them, fire proceeds from their month and devours their enemies. And if anyone wants to harm them they will be killed in this manner. These have power to shut heaven, so that no rain falls in the days of their prophecy; and they have power over water to turn them to blood, and to strike the earth with all plagues, as often as they desire. **(The book of Revelation Chapter11 verses 3-6).**

The Bible prophecy about nuclear war: At some point, probably near the end of three-and-half-year Great Tribulation, the Antichrist and ten "kings who join forces with him, will destroy the mysterious "Babylon the Great, "in what sounds like a nuclear holocaust. Scripture indicates that this Babylon is not the ancient city or empire by that name, but rather the great worldwide, materialistic, capitalistic system, epitomized by—but not limited to—the USA. According to the visions of the prophet Daniel, the ten kings who join with the Antichrist emerge from the ancient Roman Empire and thus could possibly be Europe. And I saw a woman sitting on a scarlet beast which was full of names of blasphemy, having seven heads and ten horns—And on her forehead a name was written:

"Mystery, Babylon the Great, the mother of Harlots and of the Abominations of the Earth: I saw the woman, drunk with the blood of the saints and with the blood of the martyrs of Jesus: (Revelation chapter 17 verses3-6). The ten horns which you saw are ten kings who have received no kingdom as yet, but they received authority for one hour as kings with the beast. These are of one mind, and they will give their power and authority to the beast—these will hate the harlot, make her desolate and naked, eat her flesh and burn her with fire. (Revelation chapter 17 verses 12-16). Therefore, her plagues will come in one day—death and morning and famine. And she will be utterly burned with fire—The kings of the earth who committed fornication and lived luxurious with her will weep and lament for her, when they see the smoke of her burning, standing at a distance for fear of her torment, saying, "Alas, Alas, that great city Babylon, that mighty city: For in one hour your judgment has come." And the merchants of the earth will weep and mourn over her, for no one buy their merchandise anymore: Alas, Alas, that great city, in which all that had ships on the sea became rich by her wealth. For in one hour she is made desolate." (Revelation Chapter 18 verses 8-19). The Second Coming of Jesus Christ; At the end of the Great Tribulation, Jesus will return. The sun and the moon will be darkened, but then a bright light will be seen around the world, followed by a sound of a mighty trumpet.

Jesus will be seen by everyone as he appears in the clouds of the sky surrounded by angels. Then he will rescue his followers out of this world, and they will receive new immortal bodies and be caught up from the Earth in what is called the Rapture. Scripture confirms that this event occurs "immediately after the Tribulation" and not before, as portrayed in recent popular novels and movies. Immediately after the tribulation of those days the sun will be darkened, and the moon will not give its light; the stars will fall from heaven, and the powers of heaven will be shaken. (Matthew chapter 24 verses 29). Then the seventh angel sounded: And there were loud voices in heaven, saying, "the kingdom of this world has become the Kingdoms of our Lord Jesus Christ, and he shall reign forever and ever." (Revelation chapter 11 verses 15). Then I looked, and behold, a white cloud, and on the cloud sat One like the Son of Man, having on his head a golden crown. (Revelation chapter 14 verses 14-16). Then the signs of the Son of Man will appear in heaven, and then all the tribes of the earth will mourn, and they will see the Son of Man coming on the clouds of heaven with power and great glory. And he will send his angels with great sound of trumpet, and they will gather together his elect from the four winds, from one end of heaven to the other. (Matthew chapter 24 verses30-31). Behold, I tell you a mystery: We shall not all die, but we shall all be changed—in a moment, in the twinkling of an eye, at the last trumpet.

For the trumpet will sound, and the dead will be raised incorruptible, and we shall be changed. (1 Corinthians chapter 15 verses 51-52). For the Lord will descend from heaven with a shout, with the voice of an archangel, and with the trumpet of God. And the dead in Christ will rise first. Then we who are alive and remain shall be caught up together with him in the clouds to meet the Lord in the air. And thus, we shall always be with the Lord. (1Thessalonians chapter 4 verses 16-18). **The Marriage Supper of the Lamb:** In Heaven, a celebration is then held called the Marriage Supper of the Lamb. One of the titles of Jesus is the Lamb of God,(John 1:29) and His bride is all those who believe on him(Romans 7:4) The marital metaphor is used in the Bible to describe the intimate spiritual unity between Christ and his people, and the frequency of the loving union of heart, mind, and spirit that accompanies this relationship. During this Marriage Supper, Jesus will unite with those he rescued in the Rapture, and his followers throughout the ages, and at his judgment seat he will reward them with eternal crown of life. And I heard, as it were, the voice of a great multitude, as the sound of many waters and as the sound of mighty thundering, saying, "Alleluia; For the Lord God Omnipotent reigns. Let us be glad and rejoice and give him glory, for the marriage of the Lamb has come, and his wife has made herself ready. And to her it was granted be arrayed in fine linen, clean and bright, for the fine linen is the righteous acts of the saints. Then he said to me, "Write" Blessed are those who are called to the marriage supper of the Lamb (Revelation 19 verses 6-9). For the son of Man (Jesus) will come in the glory of his father with his angels, and then He will reward each according to his works Matthew 16: 27: At the same time the wrath of God will be poured upon the whole world.

CHAPTER 18

American Government (Citizenship)

Principles of American Democracy;

What is the law of the land? The Constitutions:

What does the Constitution do? Sets up the government, defines the government, and protects basic rights of Americans.

The idea of self-government is in the first three words of the Constitution. What are these words? We the People:

What is an amendment? A change (to the Constitution) an addition (to the constitution)

What do we call the first ten amendments to the Constitution? The Bill of Rights

What is one right or freedom from the First Amendment? Speech, religion, assembly, press, petition the government

How many amendments does the Constitution have? Twenty-seven (27): What did the Declaration of Independence do? Announce our Independence (from Great Britain), declared our Independence (from Great Britain), said that United States is free (from Great Britain)

What is freedom of religion? You can practice any religion, or not practice a religion

What are two rights in the Declaration of Independence? Life, liberty, pursuit of happiness

What is the economic system in the United States? Capitalist economy, market economy

What is the "rule of law"? Everyone must follow the law, Leaders must obey the law, Government must obey the law, No one is above the law

System of American Government

Name one branch or part of the government. Congress, Legislative, President, Executive, the courts, Judicial

What stops one branch of government from becoming too powerful? Checks and balances, separation of powers

Who is in charge of the executive branch? The President

Who makes Federal laws? Congress, Senate and House (of Representative) (U.S or national) legislature

What are the two parts of the U.S. Congress? The Senate and House (of Representative)

How many U. S Senators are there? One hundred (100)

We elect U. S Senator for how many years? Six (6) years

Who is one of your states U. S Senators now?

The house of Representative has how many voting members? Four hundred and thirty-five (435)

We elect a U S Representative for how many years? Two (2) years

Name your U S Representative?

Who does a U S Senator represent? All people of the State

Why do some States have more Representative than other States? Because (of the state's population, because (they have more people, because (some states have more people

We elect a President for how many years? Four (4) years

In what month do we vote for President? November

What is the name of the President of the United States now? Barack Obama;

What is the name of the Vice President of the United States now? Joseph R Biden Jr. Joe Biden. Biden.

If the President can no longer serve, who becomes President? The Vice President

If both the President and the Vice President can no longer serve, who becomes President? The speaker of the House

Who is the Commander in Chief of the military? The President

Who signs bills to become laws? The President

Who vetoes bills? The President

What does the President's Cabinet do? Advises the President

What are two Cabinet-level positions? Secretary of Agriculture, Secretary of Commerce, Secretary of Defense, Secretary of Education, Secretary of Energy, Secretary of Health and Human Services, Secretary of Homeland Security, Secretary of Housing and Urban Development, Secretary of the interior, Secretary of labor, Secretary of States, Secretary of Transportation, Secretary of the Treasury, Secretary of Veterans Affairs, Attorney General, Vice President.

What does the judicial branch do? Reviews laws, explains laws, resolves disputes (disagreements), decides if a law goes against the Constitution

What is the highest court in the United States? The Supreme Court

How many justices are on the Supreme Court? Nine (9)

Who is the Chief Justice of the United States now? John Roberts (John G Roberts Jr.)

Under our Constitution, some powers belong to the federal government. What is one power of the federal government? To print money, to declare war, to create an army, to make treaties

Under our Constitution, some powers belong to the states. What is one of the powers of the States? Provide schooling and education, provide protection (police), provide safety (fire departments), give a driver's license, approve zoning and land use

Who is the governor of your states now? -------

What is the capital of your states--------?

What are the two major political parties in the United States? Democratic and Republican

What is the political party of the President now? Democratic (Party)

What is the name of the Speaker of the House of Representatives now? John Boehner

Rights and Responsibilities

There are four amendments to the Constitution about who can vote. Describe one of them. Citizens eighteen

(18) and older (can vote), you don't have to pay (a poll tax) to vote, Any citizen can vote(Women and Men can vote), A male citizen of any race (can vote),

What is one responsibility that is only for United States citizen? Vote in a federal election, run for federal office

What are two rights only for United States? Freedom of expression: freedom of speech, freedom of assembly, freedom to petition the government, freedom of worship, the rights to bear arms.

What do you show loyalty to when we say the Pledge of Allegiance? The United States, the flag

What is one promise you make when you become a United States citizen? Give up loyalty to other countries, defend the Constitution and laws of the United States, obey the laws of the United States, and serve in the U.S military (if needed), serve (do important work for(the nation(if needed), be loyal to the United States.

How old do citizens have to be to vote for President? Eighteen (18) and older

What are two ways that Americans can participate in their democracy? Vote, join a political party, help with a

Campaign, join a civic group, join a community group, give an elected official your opinion on an issue, call Senators and Representatives, publicly support or oppose an issue or policy, write to a newspaper

When must all men register for the Selective Service? At eighteen (18) between (18) and twenty-six (26)

AMERICAN HISTORY

Colonial Period and Independence

What is one reason colonists came to America? Freedom, political liberty, religious freedom, economic opportunity, practice their religion, escape persecution

Who lived in America before the Europeans arrived? American Indians, Native Americans

What group of people was taken to America and sold as slaves? Africans, people from Africa

Why did the colonists fight the British? Because of high taxes (taxation without representation), because the British army stayed in their houses (boarding, quartering) because they did not have self-government

Who wrote the Declaration of Independence? Thomas Jefferson

When was the Declaration of Independence adopted? July 4, 1776

There were 13 original states. Name them, New Hampshire, Massachusetts, Rhode Island, Connecticut, New York, New

Jersey, Pennsylvania, Delaware, Maryland, Virginia, North Carolina, South Carolina, Georgia

What happened at the Constitutional Convention? The Constitution was written, The Founding Fathers wrote the Constitution.

When was the Constitution written? 1787

The Federalist Papers supported the passage of the U.S Constitution. Name one of the writers. James Madison, Alexander Hamilton, John Jay, Publius.

What is one thing Benjamin Franklin is famous for? U.S. diplomat, oldest member of the Constitutional Convention, first Postmaster General of the United States, writer of "Poor Richard's Almanac", started the first free libraries

Who is the "Father of Our Country"? George Washington:

What territory did the United States buy from France in 1803? The Louisiana Territory, Louisiana

Name one war fought by the United States in the 1800s. War of 1812, Mexican-American war, the Civil War, Spanish-American War

Name the U S war between the North and the South. The Civil War, the War Between the States

Name one problem that led the Civil War. Slavery, economic reasons, states' rights

What was one important thing that Abraham Lincoln did? Freed the slaves (Emancipation Proclamation), saved (or preserved) the Union, led the United States during the Civil War

What did the Emancipation Proclamation do? Freed the slaves, freed slaves in the Confederacy, freed slaves in the Confederate states, freed slaves in most Southern states

What did Susan B. Anthony do? Fought for women's rights, fought for civil rights

Recent American History and Other Important Historical Information: Name one war fought by the United States in the 1900s. World War I, World War II, , Korean War, Vietnam War, Persian Gulf War

Who was the President during World War I? Woodrow Wilson

Who was the President during the Great Depression and World War II? Franklin Roosevelt

Who did the United States fight in World War II? Japan, Germany and Italy

Before he was President, Eisenhower was a general. What war was he in?

During the Cold War, what was the main concern of the United States? Commission

What movement tried to end racial discrimination? Civil rights movement

What did Martin Luther king, Jr do? Fought for civil rights, worked for equality of all Americans

What major event happened on September 11, 2001, in the United States? Terrorists attacked the United States

Geography: Name one of the two longest rivers in the United States? Missouri River), Mississippi River)

What Ocean in the West Coast of the United States? Pacific Ocean: What Ocean is on the East Coast of the United States? Atlantic Ocean

When do we celebrate Independence Day? July 4th

Name two national U.S holidays New Year's day, Martin Luther King Jr, Day, Presidents day, Memorial day, , Independence day, labor day, Columbus Day, Veteran's day, Thanksgiving day, Christmas day

What is the name of the national anthem? The Star-Spangled Banner

Why does the flag have 13 stripes? Because there were 13 original colonies, because the stripes represent the 13 original colonies

Why does the flag have 50 stars? Because there is one star for each state, because each star represents a state, because there are fifty states

What is the capital of United States? Washington D. C

Where is the Statute of Liberty? New York Harbor, Liberty Island, New Jersey near New York City, at the Hudson River,

Name one state that boarders Mexico. California, Arizona, New Mexico, Texas,

Name one U. S territory. Puerto-Rico, U.S Virgin Island, American Samoa, Northern Mariana Islands, Guam

Name one state that boarders Canada. Maine, New Hampshire, Vermont, New York, Pennsylvania, Ohio, Michigan, Minnesota, North Dakota, Montana, Idaho, Washington, Alaska

Name one American Indian tribe in the United States. Cherokee, Navajo, Sioux, Chippewa, Choctaw, Pueblo, Apache, Iroquois, Creek, Blackfeet, Seminole, Cheyenne, Arawak, Shawnee, Mohegan, Hopi, Teton, Lakota, Huron, Oneida, Crow, Inuit,

CHAPTER 19

Inspiration and Encouragement

To overcome adversity, you also need words of inspiration from people who have experience adversity and overcame: **Here is the story of my Hero Steve Jobs**, the founder and CEO of Apple computer. This is a prepared text of Commence address delivered by Steve Jobs, CEO of Apple Computer and of Pixar Animation Studios, on June 12 2005. **You have got to find what you love**: Steve Jobs said, I am honored to be with you today at your commencement from one of the finest universities in the world. I never graduated from college. Truth to be told, this is the closest I have ever gotten to college graduation. Today I want to tell you three stories from my life. That is it. No big deal.

The first story is about connecting the dots. I dropped out of Reed College after the first six months, but then stayed around as a drop-in for another eighteen months or so before I really quits. So why did I drop out? It started before I was born. My biological mother was a young, unwed college graduate student, and she decided to put me up for adoption. She felt very strongly that I should be adopted by college graduates, so everything was all set for me to be adopted at birth by a lawyer and his wife. Expect that when I popped out they decided at the last minute that they really wanted a girl. So, my parents, who were on a waiting list, got a call in the middle of the night asking: "We have an unexpected baby boy; do you want him?" They said of "Course." My biological mother later found out that my mother had never graduated from college and that my father had never graduated from high school. She refused to sign the final adoption papers. She only relented a few months later when my parents promised that I would someday go to college. And seventeen years later I did go to college. But I naively chose a college that almost as expensive as Stanford, and all my working-class parents savings were being spent on my college tuition. After six months, I couldn't see the value in it. I had no idea want I wanted to do with my life and no idea how college was going to help me out. And here I was spending all the money my parents had saved their entire life. So, I decided to drop out and trust that it would all work out OK. It was pretty scary at the time but looking back it was one of the best decisions I ever made. The minute I dropped out I could stop taking the required classes that didn't interest me and begin dropping in on the ones that looked interesting. It wasn't all romantic. I dint have a dorm room, so I slept on the floor in friend's rooms, I returned coke bottles for the 5c deposits to buy food with, and I would walk the 7 miles across town every Sunday night to get one good meal a week at the Hare Krishna temple. I loved it. And much of what I stumbled into by following my curiosity and intuition turned out to be priceless later on. Let me give you one example: Reed College at that time offered perhaps the best calligraphy instruction in the country. Throughout the campus every poster, every label on every drawer, was beautiful hand calligraphic. Because I had dropped out and didn't have to take the normal classes, I decided to take a calligraphy class to learn how to do this. I learned about serif and san serif typefaces, about varying the amount of space between differ- ent letters combinations, about what makes great typography great. It was beautiful, historical, artistically subtle in a way that science can't capture, and I found it fascinating. None of this had even a hope of any practical application in my life. But ten years later when we were designing the first Macintosh computer, it all came back to me. And we designed it all into the Mac. It was the first computer with beautiful typography.

If I had never dropped in on that single course in college, the Mac would have never had a multiple typefaces or pro- portionally spaced fonts. And since Windows just copied the Mac, it is likely that no personal computer would have them. If I had never dropped out, I would have never dropped in on this calligraphy class, and personal computers might not have the wonderful typography that they do. Of course, it was impossible to connect the dots looking forward when I was in college. But it was very, very clear looking backwards ten years later. Again, you cannot connect the dots looking forward; you can only connect them looking backwards. So, you have to trust that the dots will somehow connect in your future. You have to trust in something—your gut, destiny, life, karma, whatever. This approach has never let me down, and it has made all the difference in my life. **My second story is about love and loss**. I was lucky—I found what I loved to do early in life. WOZ and I started Apple in my parent's ga- rage when I was 20. We worked hard, and in 10 years Apple had grown from just two of us in a garage into a $2 billion company with over 4000 employees. We had just released our finest creation—the Macintosh—a year earlier, and I had just turned 30. And then I got fired. How can you get fired from the company you started? Well, as Apple grew we hired someone who I thought was very talented to run the company with me, and for the first year or so things went well.

But then our visions of the future began to diverge and eventually we had a falling out. When we did, our Board of Directors sided with him. So, at 30 I was out. And very publicly out. What had been the focus of my entire adult life was gone, and it was devastating. I really didn't know what to do for a few months. I felt that I had let the future of entrepreneurs down—that I had dropped the baton as it was being passed to me. I met with David Packard and Bob Noyce and tried to apologize for screwing up so badly. I was a very public failure, and I even thought about running away from the valley. But something slowly began to dawn on me—I still love what I did. The turn of events at Apple had not changed that one bit. I had been rejected, but I was still in love. So I decided to start all over. I didn't see it then, but it turned out that getting fired from Apple was the best thing that could have ever happened to me. The heaviness of being successful was replaced by the lightness of being a beginner again, less sure about everything. It freed me to enter into one of the most creative periods of my life. During the next five years, I started a company named NeXT, another company named Pixar, and fell in love with an amazing woman who would become my wife. Pixar went on to create the world's first computer animated feature film, Toy Story, and is now the most successful animation studio in the world. In a remarkable turn of events, Apple bought NeXT, I returned to Apple, and the technology we developed at NeXT is at the heart of Apple's current renaissance.

And Laurence and I have a wonderful family together. I am pretty sure none of this would have happened if I hadn't been fired from Apple. It awful tasted medicine, but I guess the patient needed it. Sometimes life hits you in the head with a brick. Don't lose faith. I am convinced that the only thing that kept me going was that I loved what I did. You have got to find what you love. And that is as true for your work as it is for your lovers. Your work is going to fill a large part of your life, and the only way to be truly satisfied is to do what you believe is great work. And the only way to do great work is to love what you do. If you haven't found it yet, keep looking. Don't settle. As with all matters of the heart, you will know when you find it. And, like any great relationship, it just gets better and better as the years roll on. So keep looking until you find it. Don't settle. **My third story is about death.** When I was 17, I read a quote that went something like: "If you live each day as if it was your last, someday you will most certainly be right." It made an impression on me, and since then, for the past 33 years, I have looked in the mirror every morning and asked myself: "If today were the last day of my life, would I want to do what I am to do today? And whenever the answer has been "No" for too many days in a row, I know I need to change something. Remembering that I would be dead soon is the most important tool I have ever encountered to help me make the big choices in life. Because almost everything—all external expectations, all pride, all fear of embarrassment or failure-these things just fall away in the face of death, leaving only what is truly important. Remembering that you are go- ing to die is the best way I know to avoid the trap of thinking you have something to lose. You are already naked. There is no reason not to follow your heart. About a year ago I was diagnosed with cancer. I had a scan at 7:30 in the morning, and it clearly showed a tumor on my pancreas. I didn't even know what pancreas was. The doctors told me this was almost certainly a type of cancer that is incurable, and that I should expect to live no longer than three to six months. My doctor advised me to go home and get my affairs in order, which is the doctor's code for prepare to die. It means to try to tell your kids everything you thought you do have the next 10 years to tell them in just a few months. It seems to make sure everything is buttoned up so that it will be easy as possible for your family. It means to say your goodbyes. I lived with that diagnosed all the day. Later that day I had a biopsy, where they stuck an endoscope down my throat, through my stomach and into my intestines, put a needle into my pancreas and got few cells from the tumor

I was sedated, but my wife, who was there, told me that when they viewed the cells under a microscope the doctors started crying because it turned out to be a very rare form of pancreas cancer that is curable with surgery. I had the surgery and I am fine now. This was the closest I have been to facing death, and I hope it's the closest I get for a few more decades. Having lived through it, I can now say this to you with a bit more certainty than when death was a useful but purely intellectual concept: No one wants to die. Even people who want to go to heaven don't want to die to get there. And yet death is the destination we all share. No one has ever escaped it. And that is s it should be, because death is very likely the single best invention of life. It is life's change agent. It clears the old to make way for the new. Right now, the new is you, but someday not too long from now, you will gradually become the old and be cleared away. Sorry to be so dramatic, but it is quite true. Your time is limited, so don't waste it living someone else life. Don't be trapped by dogma—which is living with the results of another people's thinking. Don't let the noise of others opinions drown out your own inner voice. And most importantly, have the courage to follow your hearts and intuition. They somehow already know what you truly want to become. Everything else is secondary. When I was young, there was an amazing publication called The Whole Earth Catalog, which was one of the bibles of my generation. It was created by a fellow named Stewart Brand not far from here in Menlo Park, and he brought it to life with his poetic touch. This was in the late 1960's, before personal computers and desktop publishing, so it was all made with typewriters, scissors, and Polaroid cameras. It was sort of like Google in paperback form, 35 years before Google came along: It was idealistic, and overflowing with neat tools and great notions. Stewart and his team put several issues of the Whole Earth Catalog, and then when it had run its course, they put out a final issue. It was the mid-1970s, and I was your age. On the back cover of their final issue was a photograph of an early morning country road, the kind you might find yourself hitchhiking on if you were so adventurous. Beneath it were the words: "Stay Hungry. Stay Foolish." It was their farewell message as they signed off. Stay Hungry. Stay Foolish. And I have always wished that for myself. And now, as you graduate to begin anew, I wish that for you. Stay Hungry. Stay Foolish. Thank you all very much.

Adversity and determination: Adversity; When circumstances or situations work against you, you face adversity. Refugees from war-torn countries encounter terrible adversity. Adversity, a noun which has been a part of the English language for over 800 years, comes from the Latin adversus, literally "turned against," and figuratively "hostile or unfavorable." When things seem against you—circumstances or stoke of bad luck—you are facing adversity. Sometimes people use a form of the phrase "turning adversity into opportunity." This refers to the ability some people or companies have to take a bad situation and make it into a successful one.

Through determination you can overcome: Determination is a positive emotion that involves persevering towards a difficult goal in spite of obstacles. Determination occurs prior to goal attainment and serves to motivate behavior that will help achieve one's goal. Empirical research suggests that people consider determination to be an emotion; in other words, determination is not just a cognitive state, but rather an affective state. In the psychology literature, researchers have studied determination under other terms, including challenge and anticipatory enthusiasm; this may explain one reason for the relative lack of research on determination compared to other positive emotions. In the field of psychology, emotion research is heavily focused on negative emotions and the action tendencies that they encourage. However, recent work in positive psychology incorporates the study of determination as a positive emotion that pushes individuals toward action and results in important outcomes such as perseverance and the development of coping mechanisms. There are major theories for example: **Self-determination theory** (SDT) is a theory of motivation. SDT focuses on the interplay between individual personalities and experiences in social contexts that result in motivations of the autonomous and controlled kind. Ultimately, social environments seem to have a profound effect on both intrinsic and extrinsic motivation and self-regulation.

More specifically, self-determination theory proposes that social and cultural factors influence an individual's sense of personal volition and initiative in regards to goals, performance and well-being. High levels of determination and personal volition are supported by conditions that foster autonomy (e.g. individual has multiple options/choices), competence (e.g. positive feedback) and relatedness (e.g. stable connection to the group an individual is working within). **Biopsychosocial model**: Emotions researchers continue to search for specific physiological patterns associated with discrete positive emotions; however, the frequent blending of emotions makes drawing such distinctions difficult. In relation to challenge and determination, psychologists have concluded it is best to focus on physiological activation in relation to the individuals intended.

CHAPTER 20

How to Overcome
Anxiety and Depression

Anxiety from a Latin word Anxietas; Distress or uneasiness caused by fear of danger or misfortune. A state of apprehension and psychic tension occurring in some forms of mental disorder: A states of uneasiness and apprehension, as about future uncertainties. (Psychiatry) A state of apprehension, uncertainty, and fear resulting from the anticipation of a realistic or fantasized threatening event or situation, often impairing physical and psychological functioning: (Psychology) psychol a state of intense apprehension or worry often accompanied physical symptoms such as shaking, intense feelings in the gut; etc., common in mental illness or after a very distressing experience.

Emotion, nervousness, and tension: Anxiety is general term for several disorders that cause, nervousness, fear, apprehension, and worrying. These disorders affect how we feel and behave, and they can manifest real physical symptoms. Anxiety is an unpleasant state of inner turmoil, accompanied by nervous behavior, such as pacing back and forth, somatic complaints and rumination. It is the subjectively unpleasant feelings of dread over anticipated events, such as the feeling of imminent death. Anxiety is not the same as fear, which is response to a real or perceived immediate threat whereas anxiety is the expectation of future threat.

Anxiety is a feeling of fear, worry, and uneasiness, usually generalized and unfocused as an overreaction to a situation that is only subjectively seen as menacing. It is often accompanied by muscular tension, restlessness, fatigue and problems in concentration. Anxiety can be appropriate, but when it is too much and continues too long, the individual may suffer from anxiety disorder. People facing anxiety may withdraw from situations which have provoked anxiety in the past. There are different types of anxiety. **What is Generalized Anxiety Disorder (GAD)?** **Generalized Anxiety Disorder GAD** is a chronic disorder characterized by excessive, long-lasting anxiety and worry about nonspecific life events, objects, and situations.

GAD sufferers often feel afraid and worry about health, money, family, work, or school, but they have trouble both identifying the specific fear and controlling the worries. Their fear is usually unrealistic or out of proportion with what may be expected in their situation. Sufferers expect failure and disaster to the point that it interferes with daily functions like work, school, social activities, and relationships. **What is Panic Disorder? Panic Disorder** is a type of anxiety characterized by brief or sudden attacks of intense terror and apprehension that leads to shaking, confusion, dizziness, nausea, and difficulty breathing. Panic attacks tend to rise abruptly and peak after 10 minutes, but then then may last for hours.

Panic disorders usually occur after frightening experiences or prolonged stress, but they can be spontaneous as well. A panic attack may lead an individual to be acutely aware of any change in normal body function, interpreting it as a life-threatening illness-hypervigilance followed by hypochondriasis. In addition, panic attacks lead sufferer to expect future attacks, which may cause drastic behavioral changes in order to avoid these attacks. **What is a Phobia? A Phobia** is an irrational fear and avoidance of an object or situation; Phobias are different from generalized anxiety disorders because phobia has a fear response identified with a specific cause. The fear may be acknowledged as irrational or unnecessary, but the person is still unable to control the anxiety that results.

Stimuli for phobia may be as varied as situations, animals, or everyday objects. For example, agoraphobia occurs when one avoids a place or situation to avoid an anxiety or panic attack. Agoraphobics will situate themselves so that escape will not be difficult or embarrassing, and they will change their behavior to reduce anxiety about being able to escape. **What is Social Anxiety Disorder? Social Anxiety Disorder** is a type of social phobia characterized by a fear of being negatively judged by others or fear of public embarrassment due to impulsive actions. This includes feelings such as stage fright, a fear of intimacy, and a fear of humiliation. This disorder can cause people to avoid public situations and human contact to the point that normal life is rendered impossible. **What is Obsessive-Compulsive Disorder (OCD) Obsessive- Compulsive Disorder (OCD)** is an anxiety disorder characterized by thoughts or actions that are repetitive, distressing, and intrusive. OCD suffers usually know that their compulsions are unreasonable or irrational, but they deserve to alleviate their anxiety. Often, the logic of someone with OCD will appear superstitious, such as insistence in walking a certain pattern. OCD sufferers may obsessively clean personal items or hands or constantly check locks, stoves, or light switches. **What is Post-Traumatic Stress Disorder (PTSD)? Post-Traumatic Stress Disorder (PTSD)** is anxiety that results from previous trauma such as military combat, rape, hostage situations, or a serious accident. PTSD often leads to flashbacks and behavioral changes in order to avoid certain stimuli. **What is Separation Anxiety Disorder? Separation Anxiety Disorder** is characterized by high levels of anxiety when separated from a person or place that provides feelings of security or safety. Sometimes separation result in panic and it is considered a disorder when the response is excessive or inappropriate.

What are the causes of Anxiety?

Anxiety disorders may be caused by environmental factors, medical factors, genetics, brain chemistry, substance abuse, or combination of these. It is most commonly triggered by the stress in our lives. Usually anxiety is a response to outside forces, but it is possible that we make ourselves anxious with "negative self-talk"- a habit of always telling ourselves the worse will happen. **Environmental and external factors:** Environmental factors that are known to cause several types of anxiety include: Trauma from events such as abuse, victimization, or the death of a loved one. Stress in personal relationship, marriage, friendship, divorce. Stress at work. Stress from school. Stress about finances and money. Stress from a natural disaster. Lack of oxygen in high altitude:

Medical factors: Anxiety is associated with medical factors such as anemia, asthma, infections and several heart conditions. Some medically-related causes of anxiety include: Stress from a serious medical illness. Side effects of medication: Symptoms of a medical illness. Lack of oxygen from emphysema, or pulmonary embolism (a blood clot in the lung) Substance use and abuse: It is estimated that about half of patients who utilize mental health services for anxiety disorders such as GAD, panic disorder, or social phobia are doing so because of alcohol or benzodiazepine dependence.

More generally anxiety is also know to result from: Intoxication from an illicit drug, such as cocaine or amphetamines. With draw from illicit drug, such as heroin or from prescription drugs like Vicodin, benzodiazepines, or barbiturates. **Genetics:** It has been suggested by some researchers that a family history of anxiety increases the likelihood that a person will develop it. That is, some people may have a genetic predisposition that gives them a greater chance of suffering from anxiety disorders. **Brain chemistry**; Research has shown that people with abnormal levels of certain neurotransmitters in the brain are more likely to suffer from generalized anxiety disorder. When neurotransmitters are not working properly, the brain internal communication network breaks down, and the brain may react in an inappropriate way in some situations. This can lead to anxiety.

10 Solutions to overcome Anxiety and Depression: Over 40 million Americans report feelings of anxiety; that's over 18 percent of the adults' population. There is always a battle going on in the mind from the moment you wake up until the moment you go back to sleep. To engage in this battle of the mind, you must protect yourself with armor against ongoing negative intrusive thoughts that flood the brain, while sending my prefrontal cortex—the home of logical thought—the green light to make decisions and to take charge of my brain's limbic system (the emotional hub) which is called the **"Renewal of your mind":** Meaning by replacing negative thought of defeat and hopelessness and to think differently and positively in your mind.

That is, before the amygdala (fear center) spazzes out. I spend more time and energy in chasing and maintaining good health than I do in any other aspect of my life—marriage, family, work—because I know that everything meaningful and good around me depends on a stable base. I hope that one day I won't have to fight so hard for my sanity. However, until then, here is a list of things I do every day to overcome Anxiety and Depression. (1) Exercise is the most powerful weapon the demons. (2) Record your joy (3) List your accomplishments (4) Laughter (5) Meditation (6) Take DHA and Vitamins recommended (7) drink a power smoothie (8) Avoid sugar and grains (9) Prayers; you should pray: 10 consult your doctor:

CHAPTER 21

Nelson Mandela Turned Prison into Palace

Nelson Mandela turned prison in palace: after 27 years in prison and he became the president of South Africa: President Nelson Mandela was born in 18th July 1918. He was a South African anti-apartheid revolutionary, politician and philanthropist who served as President of South Africa from 1994 to 1999. He was South Africa's first black chief executive, and the first elected in a fully representative democratic election. His government focused on dismantling the legacy of apartheid through tackling institutionalized racism, poverty and inequality, and fostering racial reconciliation. Politically an African nationalist and democratic socialist, he served as President of the African National Congress (ANC) from1991 to 1997. Internationally, Mandela was secretary general of the Non-Aligned Movement from 1998 to 1999.

Nelson was born to the Thembu royal family; Mandela attended the Fort Hare University and the University of Witwatersrand, where he studied law. Living in Johannesburg, he became involved in anti-colonial politics, joining ANC and becoming a founding member of its Youth League. After the Afrikaner minority government of the National Party established apartheid in 1948, he rose to prominence in the ANC's 1952 Defiance Campaign, was appointed superintendent of the organization's Transvaal chapter and presided over the 1955 Congress of the People. Working as a lawyer, he was repeatedly arrested for seditious activities and, with the ANC leadership, was unsuccessfully prosecuted in the Treason Trial from 1956 to 1961. Influenced by Marxism, he secretly joined the South African Communist Party (SACP) and sat in its central Committee. Although in initially committed to non-violent protest, in association with the SACP he co-founded the militant Umkhonto we Sizwe (MK) in 1961, leading sabotage campaign against the apartheid government. In 1962, he was arrested, convicted of conspiracy to overthrow the state, and sentenced to life imprisonment in the Rivonia Trial.

Mandela served 27 years in prison, initially on Robben Island, and later in Pollsmoor Prison and Victor Verster Prison. An International campaign lobbied for his release, which was granted in 1990 amid escalating civil strife. Mandela joined negotiations with Nationalist President F. W. de Klerk to abolish apartheid and establish multiracial elections in 1994, in which he led the ANC to victory and became South Africa's first black president. He published his autobiography in 1995. During his tenure in the Government of National Unity he invited other political parties to join the cabinet and promulgated a new constitution. He also created the Truth and Reconciliation Commission to investigate past human rights abuses. While continuing the former government's liberal economic policy, his administration also introduced measures to encourage land reform, combat poverty, and expand health-care services. Internationally, he acted as a mediator between Libya and the United Kingdom in the Pan Am Flight 103 bombing trial and oversaw military intervention in Lesotho. He declined to run for a second term, and was succeeded by his deputy, Thabo Mbeki. Mandela became an elder states-man, focusing on charitable work in combating poverty and HIV/AIDS through the Nelson Mandela Foundation. Mandela was a controversial figure for much of his life. Denounced as a communist terrorist by critics, he nevertheless gained inter-national acclaim for his activism, having received more than 250 honors, including the 1993 Nobel Peace Prize, the US Presidential Medal of Freedom, and the Soviet Order of Lenin.

He is held in deep respect within South Africa, where he is often referred to by his Xhosa clan name, Madiba, or as Tata (Father) he is often described as the "Father of the Nation": **Nelson Mandela said "I have cherished the ideal of a demo-cratic and free society in which all persons will live together in harmony and with equal opportunities. It is an ideal for which I hope to live for and to see realized. But, My Lord, if it needs be, it is an ideal for which I am prepared to die."**

Jesus Triumphant Entry into Jerusalem: As Jesus and his dis-ciples approached Jerusalem; they came to Bethphage at the Mount of Olives. There Jesus sent two of his disciples on ahead with these instructions: Go to the village there ahead of you, and at once you will find a donkey tied up with her colt beside her. Untie them and bring them to me. And if anyone says anything, tell him, "The Master needs them, and then he will let them go at once. "This happened in order to make come true what the prophet had said: Tell the city of Zion,

Look, your King is coming to you. He is humble and rides on a donkey and on a colt, the foal of a donkey. So the disciple went and did what Jesus had told them to do: they brought the donkey and the colt, threw their cloaks over them, and Jesus got on.

A large crowd of people spread their cloaks on the road while others cut branches from the trees and spread them on the road. The crowds walking in front of Jesus and those walking behind began to shout, "Praise to David's son. God bless him who comes in the name of the Lord. Praise be to God. When Jesus entered into Jerusalem, the whole city was thrown into an uproar. Who is he? The people asked. This is Prophet Jesus, from Nazareth in Galilee, the crowds answered. **Jesus goes to the Temple.** Jesus went into the Temple and drove out all those who were buying and selling there. He overturned the tables of the moneychangers and the stools of those who sold pigeons, and said to them, It is written in the Scriptures that God said, My Temple will be called a house of prayer. But you are making it a hideout for thieves. The blind and the crippled came to him in the Temple and he healed them. The chief priests and the teachers of the Law became angry with him when they saw the wonderful things he was doing and the children shouting in the Temple, "Praise to David's son. So they ask Jesus do you hear what they are saying. ? Indeed, I do, answered Jesus. "Haven't you ever read this Scripture? You have trained children and babies to offer perfect praise. Jesus left them and went out of the city to Bethany, where he spent the night.

Jesus Curses the Fig Tree: On his way back to the city early next morning, Jesus was hungry. He saw a fig tree by the sides of the roads and went to it but found nothing on it except leaves. So, he said to the fig tree, you will never again bear fruits. At once the fig tree dried up. The disciples saw this and were astounded. How did the fig tree dry up quickly? They asked. **Jesus answered, I assure you that if you believe and do not doubt, and you will be able to do what I have done to this fig tree. And not only this, but you will be able to say to this hill: Get up and throw yourself in the sea and it will. If you believe, you will receive whatever you ask for in prayer.**

The Final Judgment: When the Son of Man comes as a King and all the angels with him, he will sit on his royal throne, and the people of all the nations will be gathered before him. Then he will divide them into two groups, just as a shepherd separate the sheep from the goats. He will put the righteous people at his right and others at his left. Then the King will say to the people on his right, Come, you that are blessed by my father. Come and possess the Kingdom which has been prepared for you ever since the creation of the world. I was hungry and you fed me. Thirsty and you gave me a drink: I was a stranger and you receive me to your homes: naked and you clothed me. I was sick and you took care of me: in prison and you visited me.

The righteous will then answer him, When, Lord, did we ever see you hungry and feed you, or thirsty and give you a drink? When did we ever see you a stranger and welcome you to our homes, or naked and clothe you? When did we ever see you sick or in prison, and visit you? The King will reply, I tell you, whenever you did this for one of the least important of these followers of mine, you did it for me. Then he will say to those on his left, away from me, you that are under God's curse.

Away to the eternal fire prepared for the Devil and his angels. I was hungry, but you would not feed me, thirsty but you
would not give me a drink: I was a stranger but you would not
welcome me in your homes, naked but you would not clothe
me: I was sick and in prison but you would not take care of
me. Then they will answer him, When, Lord, did we ever see
you hungry or thirsty, or a stranger or naked, or sick or in
prison, and we would not help you? The King will reply, I tell
you whenever you refused to help one of these least important ones, you refused to help me: These, then will be sent off
to eternal punishment, but the righteous will go to eternal life

CHAPTER 22

The Plot to Kill Jesus

The Plot against Jesus: When Jesus had finished teaching all these things, he said to his disciples: In two days, as you know, it will be the Passover Festival, and the Son of Man will be handed over to be crucified. Then the chief priests and the elders met together in the palace of Caiaphas, the High Priest, and made plans to arrest Jesus secretly and put him to death. We must not do during the festival, they said, or the people will riot. **Jesus is Anointed at Bethany** Jesus was in Bethany at the house of Simon, a man who had suffered from a dreaded skin disease. While Jesus was eating, a woman came to him with an alabaster jar filled with an expensive perfume, which she poured on his head. The disciples saw this and became angry. Why all these wastes? They asked. This perfume could have been sold for a large amount and money given to the poor. Jesus knew what they were saying, and so he said to them: Why are you bothering this woman? It is a fine and a beautiful thing she has done for me. You will always have poor people with you, but you will not always have me. What she did was to pour this perfume on my body to get me ready for burial. Now, I assure you that wherever this gospel is preached all over the world, what she has done will be told in memory of her. **Judas agrees to betray Jesus:** Then one of the twelve disciples—the one named Judas Iscariot—went to the chief priests and asked, what will you give to me if I betray Jesus to you? They counted out thirty silver coins and gave them to him. From then on Judas was looking for a good chance to hand over Jesus to them. **Jesus eats the Passover meal with his Disciples** On the first day of the Festival of Unleavened bread the disciples came to Jesus and asked him, where do you want us to get the Passover meal ready for you? Go to a certain man in the city, he said to them, and tell him: The teacher says: My hour has come; my disciples and I will celebrate the Passover at your house. The disciple did as Jesus had told them and prepared the Passover meal. When it was evening, Jesus and the twelve disciples sat down to eat. During the meal Jesus said, I tell you one of you will betray me. The disciples were very upset and began to ask him, one after the other, surely the Lord you don't mean me? Jesus answered one who dips his bread in the dish with me will betray me. The Son of Man will die as the Scriptures say he will, but how terrible for that man who will betray the Son of Man. It would have been better for that man if he had never been born. Judas Iscariot, the traitor, spoke up. Surely teacher, you don't mean me? He asked Jesus answered, "So you say." **The Lord's Supper;** While they were eating, Jesus took a piece if bread, gave a prayer of thanks, broke it, and gave to his disciples. Take and eat it, he said; this is my body. Then he took the cup, gave thanks to God, and gave it to them. Drink it, all of you, he said; this is my blood which seals God's covenant, my blood poured out for many for the forgiveness of sins. I tell you I will never again drink this wine until the day I drink the new wine with you in my fathers in my father's kingdom. Then they sang a hymn and went out to Mount Olives. **Jesus Predicts Peter' Denial;** Then Jesus said to them, "This very night all of you will run away and leave me, for the Scriptures says, God will kill the shepherd, and the sheep of the flock will be scattered. But after I am raised to life, I will go to Galilee ahead of you. Peter spoke up and said to Jesus, I will never leave you, even though all the rest do. Jesus said to Peter, I tell you that before the rooster crow tonight, you will say three times that you do not know me. Peter answered; I will never say that, even if I have to die with you. And all the other disciples said the same thing.

Jesus prays in Gethsemane, Then Jesus went with his disciples to a place called Gethsemane, and he said to them, sit here while I go over there and pray. He took with him Peter and the two sons of Zebedee. Grief and anguish came over him, and he said to them, the sorrow in my heart is so great that it almost crushes me. Stay her and keep watch with me. He went a little further on threw himself face downward on the ground, and prayed, my father, if it is possible; take this cup of suffering from me. Yet not what I want, but what you want. Then he returned to the three disciples and found them asleep; and he said to Peter, how is it that you three were not able to keep watch with me even for one hour? Keep watch and pray that you will not fall into temptation. The spirit is willing but the flesh is weak.

CHAPTER 23

The Arrest, Trials, Crucifixion of Jesus

The arrest of Jesus Christ: The arrest of Jesus is a pivotal event recorded in the canonical gospels. The event ultimately leads, in the Gospel account, to Jesus crucifixion. Jesus was arrested by the Temple guards of Sanhedrin in the Garden of Gethsemane, shortly after the Last Supper (during which Jesus gave his final sermon) and immediately after the kiss of Judas, which is traditionally said to have been an act of betrayal. The arrest led immediately to his trial before the Sanhedrin, during which they condemned Jesus to death. In Christian theology, the events from the Last Supper until the crucifixion and the resurrection of Jesus are referred to as the Passion. In the New Testament, all four Gospels conclude with an extended narrative of Jesus arrest, trial, crucifixion, burial, and resurrection. In each Gospel, these five events in the life of Jesus are treated with more intense detail than any other portion of that Gospel's narrative. Scholars note that the reader receives an almost hour-by-hour account of what is happening; According to the canonical gospels, after the Last Supper,

Jesus and his disciples went out to Gethsemane, a garden lo-
cated at the edge of the Kidron Valley, thought by scholars to
probably have been an Olive grove. Once there, he described
as leaving the group so that he can pray privately. The synoptic state that Jesus asked God that his burden be taken from
him, and requested not toned to undergo the events that he
was due to, though giving the final choice to God to God.
Luke state that an angel appeared and strengthened Jesus,
who then returned to his disciples. The synoptic state that the
three disciples that were with Jesus had fallen asleep, and
that Jesus criticized them for failing to stay awake even for
an hour, suggesting that they pray so that they could avoid
temptation. At that point, Judas gave Jesus a kiss, as a pre-
arranged sign to those that had accompanied Judas as to who
Jesus was. Having been identified, the officers arrested Jesus,
although one of Jesus disciples thought to stop them with a
sword but cut off the ear of one of the arresting officers. The
Gospel of John specifies that it had been Simon Peter who had
cut off the ear of Malchus, the servant of Caiaphas, the high
priest. Luke adds that Jesus healed the wound. John, Matthew
and Luke state that Jesus criticized the violent act, insisting
that they do not resist Jesus arrest: In Matthew, Jesus made the
well-known statement "all who live by the sword, shall die by
the sword. The account in the Gospel of John differs from that
of the synoptic: only in John do Roman soldiers help to carry out the arrest. Judas leads the arresting party to Jesus, but
rather than Judas pointing out Jesus, John has Jesus himself,
knowing all that was to happen to him, "ask them whom they
are looking for; when they say: Jesus of Nazareth, he replies
I am he "at which point all members of the arrest party went
backward and fell to the ground.

The Trials of Jesus Christ: The Sanhedrin trial of Jesus refers to the trials of Jesus before the Sanhedrin (a Jewish judicial body) following his arrest in Jerusalem and prior to his dispensation by Pontius Pilate. It is an event reported by all four Canonical gospels of the New testament, although John's gospel does not explicitly mention a Sanhedrin trial in this context; Jesus is generally quiet, does not mount a defense, and rarely responds to the accusations, but is condemned by the Jewish authorities when he will not deny that he is the Son of God. The Jewish leaders then take Jesus to Pontius Pilate, the governor of Roman Judea, and ask for the death sentence for claiming to be the king of the Jews.

The trial is depicted in the Gospel accounts is temporary placed informally on Thursday night and then again formally on Friday morning; In the narrative of the canonical gospels, after the betrayal and arrest of Jesus, he is taken to the Sanhedrin. From a historical perspective, in the era in which the narrative is set, the Sanhedrin body was an ad hoc gathering, rather than a fixed court. In four canonical gospels, Jesus is tried and condemned by the Sanhedrin, mocked and beaten and is condemned for making the claim of being the son God. Although the Gospel accounts vary with respect to various details, they agree on the general character and overall structure of the trials of Jesus. Matthew Chapter 26 verses 57 states that Jesus was taken to the house of Caiaphas the high priest, where the scribes and the elders were gathered together: Matthew 27:1 adds that, the nest morning, the priests held another meeting. Mark 14:53 states that Jesus was taken that night to the high priest (without naming the high priest), where the Chief priest and all the elders gathered, and Mark 15:1 adds that another consultation was held among the priests the next morning. Luke 22:54 states that Jesus was taken to "the high priest's house" (without naming the priest) where he was mocked and beaten that night. It is added in 22:66 that, as soon as it was day, the chief priests and the scribes gathered together and led Jesus away into their council.

In John 18:12-14, however, Jesus is first taken to Annas, the father in-law of Caiaphas, who was the high priest at that time. Annas is believed to have been the former high priest, and it appears that Caiaphas sought Annas confirmation of Caiaphas actions. In 18:24, Jesus is sent from Annas to Caiaphas the high priest, and 18;28 states that, in the morning, Jesus was led from Caiaphas to Pontius Pilate in the Praetorium. In all four Gospel accounts, the trial of Jesus before the priests and scribes is interleaved, with the Denial of Peter narrative, where Apostle Peter who has followed Jesus denies knowing him three times. Luke 22:61 states that as Jesus was bound and standing at the priest's house Peter was in the courtyard. Jesus turned and looked straight at him, and Peter remembered the words Jesus

had spoken to him: "Before the rooster crows today, you will disown me three times. In the Gospel accounts, Jesus speaks very little, and gives very infrequent and indirect answers to the questions of the priests, prompting an officer to slap him. In Matthew 26:62, the lack of response from Jesus prompts the high priests to ask him: "answerers thou nothing? In the Gospel accounts the men that hold Jesus at the high priest's house mock, blindfold, insult and beat him, at times slapping him and asking him to guess who had hit him that time. Mark 14:55-59 states that the chief priests sought witness against Jesus to put him to death but did not find any, so they arranged false witness against him, but their witnesses did not agree together. Mark 14:61 states that the high priest then asked Jesus: "Art thou the Christ, the Son of the Blessed?

And Jesus said, "I am" at which point the high priest tore his robe in anger and accused Jesus of blasphemy. In Matthew 26:63, the high priest asks: "tell us whether you are the Christ, the Son of God." Jesus responds "You have said it," prompting the high priest to tear his own robe. IN Luke 22:67, Jesus is asked: "If thou art the Christ, tell us. But he said unto them, If I tell you, ye will not believe" But in 22:70, when asked, "Are you then the Son of God? Jesus answers "You say I am" affirming the title Son of God. At that point the priests say "What further need have we of witness? For ourselves have heard from his mouth" and they decide to condemn Jesus. Thereafter in Pilate's court, the Jewish elders ask Pontius Pilate to judge and condemn Jesus—accusing him of claiming to be the king of the Jews.

The Crucifixion of Jesus Christ: Crucifixion is a form of slow and painful execution in which the victim is tied or nailed to a large wooden cross and left to hang until dead. It is principally known from antiquity but remains in occasional use in some countries. The Crucifixion of Jesus occurred during the 1st century AD, most probably between the years 30 and 33. According to the accounts in the New Testament, Jesus whom Christians believe to be the Son of God as well as the Messiah was arrested, tried, and sentenced by Pontius Pilates to be scourged, and finally crucified. The English term cross derives from the Latin word crux. The Latin term crux literally means in general, a tree, frame, or other wooden instruments of execution, on which criminals were impaled or hanged, and in particular, a cross.

The English term crucifix derives from the Latin crucifixus or cruci fixus, past participle passive of crucifigere or cruci fige-re, meaning "to crucify" or "to fasten to a cross. Crucifixion was often performed to terrorize and dissuade its witnesses from perpetrating particularly heinous crimes. Victims were left on display after death as warnings to others who might attempt dissent. Crucifixion was usually intended to provide a death that was particularly slow, painful (hence the term excruciating, literally "out of crucifying), gruesome, humiliat-ing, and public, using whatever means were most expedient for that goal. Crucifixion methods varied considerably with location and time period. The Greek and Latin words corre-sponding to "crucifixion" applied to many different forms of painful execution, from impaling on a stake to affixing to a tree, to an upright pole (a crux simplex) or to a combination of an upright (in Latin, stripes) and a crossbeam (in Latin, patibu-lum). In some cases, the condemned was forced to carry the crossbeam to the place of execution. **Path to the crucifixion:** The three Synoptic Gospels refer to a man called Simon of Cyrene who is made to carry the cross, while in the Gospel of John, Jesus is said to bear his own cross. Luke's gospel also de-scribes an interaction between Jesus and the women among the crowd of mourners following him, quoting Jesus as saying "Daughters of Jerusalem, do not weep for me, but weep for yourself and for your children.

For behold, the days are coming when they will say, blessed are the barren woman and the wombs that never bore and the breast that never nursed:" Then they will begin to say to the mountains, fall on us and to the hills, and Cover us. For if they do these things when the wood is green, what will happen when it is dry? Luke 23:28-31. The Gospel of Luke has Jesus address these women as "daughters of Jerusalem, thus distinguishing them from the women whom the same gospel describes as "the women who had followed him from Galilee" and who were present at his crucifixion. Traditionally, the path that Jesus took is called Via Dolorosa (Latin for "Way of Grief" or Way of suffering") and is a street in old Jerusalem. The Gospel of Matthew describes many women at the crucifixion, some of whom are named in the Gospels. Apart from these women, the three synoptic Gospel speak of the presence of others: the chief priests, with the scribes and elders; two robbers crucified, one on Jesus right hand and the one on his left hand, whom the Gospel of Luke presents as the penitent thief and the impenitent thief, the soldiers", the centurion and those who were with him, keeping watch over Jesus, bystanders, the crowds that had assembled for this spectacle.; and his acquaintances. The Gospels of John also speaks of women present, but only mentions the soldiers and the disciple whom Jesus loved. The Gospels also tell of the arrival, after the death of Jesus, of Joseph of Arimathea, and Nicodemus.

Words of Jesus spoken from the cross: The New Testament gives three different accounts of the words of Jesus on the cross. In Mark 15:34 and in Matthew 27: 46 Eli, Eli, la 'ma sa: Bach: tha'ni? (Arabic for "My God, My God, why have you forsaken me?" :) This is a Quotation from Psalms 22: Luke 23:34 "Father, forgive them, for they know not what they do." Luke 23:43 Truly, I say to you, today you will be with me in Paradise. Luke 23: 46 "Father, into your hands I commit my spirit. The Gospel of Luke does not have the cry of Jesus found within Matthew and Mark, possibly playing down the suffering of Jesus and replacing the cry of desperation with one of hope and confidence, in keeping with the message of the Gospel which Jesus as dying confident that he would be vindicated as God's righteous prophet: John 19:25-27 "Woman, behold, your son:" John 19:28 "I thirst:" John 19:30 "It is finished: **Events which happened during the crucifixion of Jesus:** The synoptic report various miraculous events during the crucifixion, Mark mentions darkness in the daytime during Jesus crucifixion, and the Temple veil being torn in two when Jesus dies. Luke follows Mark as does Matthew, adding earthquake and the resurrection of dead saints. No mention any of these appears in John. Darkness: In the synoptic narrative, while Jesus is hanging on the cross, the sky over Judea (or the whole world) is darkened for three hours, from the sixth to the night hour. (noon to mid-afternoon).

Temple veil, earthquake and resurrection of dead saints: The synoptic gospels state that the veil of the temple was torn from top to bottom. According to Josephus, the curtain in Herod's temple would have been nearly 60 feet high inches thick. According to Hebrew 9:1-10 this curtain was a representative of the separation between God and man, beyond which only the high priest is permitted to pass, and then only once each year to enter into God's presence and make atonement for the sins of Israel. (Exodus 30:10) Many bible expositors agree that the rending of veil is symbolic of Jesus establishing a new and living way of access to God called the New Covenants. Hebrew 9:11-15. The Gospel of Matthew states that there were earthquakes, splitting rocks, and graves of dead saints were opened (and subsequently resurrected after the resurrection of Jesus). These resurrected saints went into the holy city and appeared to many people, but their subsequent fate is never elaborated upon Matthew 27: 51-53. In the synoptic accounts, the centurion in charge, witnessing these events, says: "Truly this was the Son of God, or truly this man was the Son of God or "Certainly this man was innocent (Matthew 27:54). Jesus death and resurrection underpin a variety of theological interpretations as to how salvation is granted to humanity. Crucifixion or (impalement): This reference is to being hanged from a tree and may be associated with lynching or traditional hanging.

CHAPTER **24**

The Resurrection
and Victory of Jesus

The resurrection of Jesus is the Christian religious believe that, after being put to death to take the punishment deserved by others for the sins of the world, Jesus rose again from the dead. it is the central tenet of Christian theology and part of the Nicene Creed: On the third day, he rose again in accordance with the scriptures. In the New Testament, after the Romans crucified Jesus, he was anointed and buried in a new tomb by Joseph of Arimathea, but God raised him from the dead and he appeared to many people over a span of forty days before he was taken to heaven, to sit at the right hand of God. Paul the Apostle declared that "Christ died for our sins according to the Scriptures.

And that he was buried and that he rose again the third day according to the Scripture." (1Cor15:14-15). Further, the chapter establishes that such belief in both the death and the resurrection of Christ is of central importance to the Christian faith. And if Christ be not raised: Paul further asserted that faith is so central to salvation that if Christ be not raised, your faith is in vain: then our preaching is in vain, and also your faith is in vain. Ye are yet in your sins. Then they also which are fallen asleep in Christ are perished. If in this life only we have hope in Christ, we are of all men most miserable. (1 Corinthian 15:17-19). Christian celebrates the resurrection of Jesus on Easter Sunday, two days after Good Friday, the day of his crucifixion. Easter's date corresponds roughly with Passover, the Jewish observance associated with the Exodus that is fixed for the night of the Full moon near the time of spring equinox. In the New Testament, all four gospels conclude with an extended narrative of Jesus's arrest, trial, crucifixion, burial and his resurrection. In each gospel, these five events in the life of Jesus are treated with more intense detail than any other portion of that gospel's narrative. Scholars note that the reader receives an almost hour by hour account of what is happening. The death and resurrection of Jesus treated as climax of the story, the point to which everything else has been moving all the while. After the death by crucifixion, Jesus was placed in a new tomb which was discovered early Sunday morning to empty. The New Testament does not include an account of the moment of resurrection. In the Eastern Church icons do not depict that moment but show the myrrh bearers and depict scenes of salvation. The major resurrection appearances of Jesus in the canonical gospels (and to a lesser extent other books of the New Testament) are reported to have occurred after his death, burial and resurrection, but prior to his ascension.

The Burial of Jesus: The synoptic gospels agree that, as the evening came after the crucifixion, Joseph of Arimathea asked Pilate for the body of Jesus, and that, after Pilate granted his request, wrapped it in linen cloth and laid it in a tomb. This was in accordance with Mosaic Law, which stated that a person hanged on a tree must not be allowed to remain there at night but should be buried before sundown. All four gospels report that women were the ones to find the tomb of Jesus empty, although the numbers varies from one (Mary Magdalene) to an unspecified number. According to Mark and Luke, the announcement of Jesus's resurrection was first made to women. According to Mark and John, Jesus actually appeared first to Mary Magdalene alone. Whereas others found woman not qualified or authorized to teach, the four Gospels have it that the risen Christ commissioned women to proclaim to men, including Peter and other apostles, the resurrection, foundation of Christianity.

Death state of Christ during the 3 days: According to the Book of Acts, the Apostle Peter delivered a sermon fifty day after the resurrection in which he stated: "Brothers, I can tell you confidently that God had promised him on oath he would place one of his descendants on his throne. Seeing what was ahead, he spoke of the resurrection of the Christ, that he was not abandoned to the grave, nor did his body see decay. God raised this Jesus to life, and we are all witnesses of the fact. As written in the book of Revelation: When I saw him, I fell at his feet as though dead. Then he placed his right hand on me and said: Do not be afraid. I am the First and the Last. I am the Living One. I was dead, and behold I am alive forever and ever. And I hold the keys of death and hades.1 Peter also states: For Christ, also hath once suffered for sins, the just for the unjust, that he might bring us to God, being put to death in the flesh, bur quickened by the spirit: By which also he went and preached unto the spirits in prison; which sometime were disobedient, when once the longsuffering of God waited in the days of Noah, while the ark was a preparing, wherein few, that is, eight souls were saved by water (1 Peter 3:18-20. That passage, along with the phrase that "his soul was not left in hell", is the basis of the statement that he descended into hell" in the Apostles Creed: (Acts 2:31). In the gospels, especially the synoptic: women play a central role as eyewitnesses at Jesus death, entombment, and in the discovery of the empty tomb. All three synoptic repeatedly make women the subject of verbs of seeing clearly presenting them as eyewitnesses.

Resurrection appearances of Jesus: After they found the empty tomb, the gospel indicates that Jesus made a series of appearance to the disciples. He was not immediately recognizable, according to Luke, although Jesus could appear and disappear, he was not a ghost. Luke insistent that the risen Christ could be touched, and he could eat, (Luke 24:39-43) He first appeared to Mary Magdalene, but she did not recognize him at first. The first two disciple to whom he first appeared, walked and talked with him for quite a while without out knowing who he was. (the road to Emmaus appearance (Luke 24: 13-32) He was made known in the breaking of the bread, when he first appeared to the disciples in the upper room; Thomas was not presents and would not believe until a later appearance where he was invited to put his finger into the holes in Jesus hands and side.

Beside the Sea of Galilee, he encourages Peter to serve his followers and to save souls (John 21:1-23)**: In 1 Corinthians 15:20-22 But Christ really has been raised from the dead. He is the first of all those who will rise. Death came because of what a man did. Rising from the dead also comes because of**

what a man did. Because of Adam, all people die. So, because of Christ all will be made alive. In the teachings of the apostolic church, the resurrection was seen as heralding a new era. Paul explains the importance of the resurrection of Jesus as the cause and basis of the hope of Christians to share a similar experience and the connection between the resurrection and redemption: The resurrection of Jesus has long been central to Christian faith and appears within diverse elements of the Christian tradition, from feast to artistic depictions to religious relics. In Christian teachings, sacraments derive their saving power from the passion and the resurrection of Christ, upon which the salvation of the world entirely depends; **Easter Celebration:** Easter, is the preeminent feast that celebrates the resurrection of Jesus, is clearly the earliest Christian festival. Since the earliest Christian times, it has focused on the redemptive act of God in the death and resurrection of Christ. Easter is linked to the Passover and Exodus from Egypt recorded in the Old Testament through the Last Supper and crucifixion that preceded the resurrection. According to the New Testament, Jesus gave the Passover meal a new meaning, as he prepared himself and his disciples for his death in the upper room during the Last Supper. He identified the loaf of bread and cup of wine as symbolizing his body soon to be sacrificed and his blood soon to be shed: or Christ our Passover lamb has been sacrificed.

The resurrection story appears in more than five locations in the Bible. In several episodes in the four Gospels Jesus foretells his coming death and resurrection, which he states is the plan of God the father. Christians view the resurrection of Jesus as part of the plan salvation and redemption by atonement for man's sin. Belief in the bodily resurrection of the dead became well established within some segments of Jewish society in the centuries leading up to the time of Christ, as recorded by Daniel 12:2 from the mid- 2nd century BC: "Many of those sleeping in the dust shall awaken, some to everlasting life, and some to everlasting peril.

Pharisees believed in the resurrection of the dead, and the Sadducees did not, The Sadducees, politically powerful religious leaders, rejected, the afterlife, angels, and demons as well as the Pharisees oral law. The Pharisees, whose views became Rabbinic Judaism: eventually won (or at least survived) this debate. The promise of a future resurrection appears in the Torah as well as in certain Jewish works, such as the life of Adam and Eve, 100 BC. Gospel narratives Mark: Just after the sunrise on the day after the Sabbath three women, Mary Magdalene, Mary the mother of James, and Salome, come to anoint Jesus body, wondering how they can roll the rock away from the tomb; but the found the rock already rolled aside and a young man in white inside; he tells them that Jesus is risen, and that they should tell Peter and the disciples that he will meet them in Galilee, just as he told you. The women run away and tell no one. Matthew: Just after sunrise on the day after the Sabbath two women, Mary Magdalene and the other Mary came to look at the tomb. Accompanied by an earthquake, an angel comes down from Heaven and rolls the rock aside from the tomb. The angel tells them not to be afraid, but to tell the disciples that Jesus is raised and will meet them in Galilee. The women are joyfully set out to tell the disciples the good news, but Jesus appears and tell them not to be afraid, and tell them that he is risen and that they should tell the disciples that they will see him in Galilee. The disciples go to Galilee, where they see Jesus. The soldiers guarding the tomb are terrified by the angel, and inform the chief priests; the priest and the elders bribe them to spread a lie that the disciples have stolen the body. And this story has been widely circulated among the Jews to this very day.

The Gospel according to Luke: Just after sunrise on the day after the Sabbath a number of women (Mary Magdalene, Joanna, and Mary the mother of James) come to anoint Jesus body. They found the stone rolled away and the tomb empty. Suddenly two men stand beside them. The men tell them Jesus is risen. The women tell the disciples, but the disciples do not believe them, except for Peter who runs to the tomb. Peter found the grave clothes in the empty tomb and goes away, wondering. The same day Jesus appears to two of his followers on the road to Emmaus. They fail to recognize him until he breaks the bread and gives thanks, and he then vanishes. The two go at once to Jerusalem where they found the disciples exclaiming over Jesus appearance to Peter. As they tell their story Jesus appears to them all. They are afraid, but he invites them to touch his body, eats with them, and explained the prophecies which are fulfilled in him Luke 24. The Gospel according to John: In the evening Jesus appears among the disciples, despite the locked doors, and gives them power over sin and forgiveness of sin. A week later he appears to doubting Thomas who has not believed, but when Thomas was instructed to touch the wounds of Jesus he says "My Lord and my God: Jesus replies: "Because you have seen me, you have believed: blessed are those who have not seen and yet have believed. John 20.

JESUS SAID WE SHOULD TAKE CARE OF HIS SHEEP: You must love God with all your heart and love your neighbor as

yourself: After this, Jesus appeared once more to his disciples at Lake Tiberias, this is how it happened. Simon Peter, Thomas (called the twin), Nathanael (the one from Cana in Galilee), the sons of Zebedee, and two other Jesus disciples were all together. Simon Peter said to others I am going for fishing, "We will come with you, they told him. So, they went out in a boat, but all that night they did not catch a thing. As the sun was rising, Jesus stood at the water's edge, but the disciples did not know that it was Jesus. Then he asked them, Young men, haven't you caught anything? Not a thing, they answered. He said to them "Throw your net out on the right side of the boat, and you will catch some. So, they threw the net out and could not pull it back in, because they have caught so many fish. The disciple whom Jesus loved said to Peter, it is the Lord. When Peter heard that it was the Lord, he wrapped his outer garment around him (for he had taken his clothes off) and jumped into the water. The other disciples came to shore in the boat, pulling the net full of fish. They were not very far from the land, about a hundred yards away. When they stepped ashore, they saw charcoal fire there with fish on it and some bread. Then Jesus said to them, "Bring some of the fish you have just caught. "Simon Peter went aboard and dragged the net ashore full of big fish, a hundred and fifty-three in all; even though there were so many, still the net did not tear. Jesus said to them come and eat. None of the disciples dared ask him, "Who are you?" because they knew it was the Lord. So, Jesus went over, took the bread, and gave it to them; he did the same with the fish. This, then, was the third time Jesus appeared to the disciples after he was raised from death. After they had eaten, Jesus said to Peter: Simon son of John do you love me more than these others do? "Yes, Lord, he answered, you know that I love you. Jesus said to him, Take care of my lambs.

A second time Jesus said to him, Simon son of John, do you love me? "Yes, Lord, he answered, you know that I love you. Jesus said to him, "Take care of my sheep". A third time Jesus said, "Simon son of John, do you love me? Peter became sad because Jesus asked him the third time. Do you love me? And so, he said to him Lord, you know everything; you know that I love you; **Jesus said to him, "Take care of my sheep**. I am telling you the truth when you were young you used to get ready and go anywhere you want to; but when you are old, you will stretch out your hands and someone else will tie you up and take you where you don't want to go. In saying this, Jesus was indicating the way in which Peter would die and bring glory to God.) Then Jesus said to him, Follow me

A CAUSE TO DIE FOR:

Whatever your purpose in life or your goal in life may be: Do what you love to do and the cause you are willing to die for. Nothing can stop you if you have a cause you are willing to die for;

By Nelson Mandela and Mahatma Gandhi

CHAPTER 25

God's Promise is Received Through Faith

When God promised Abraham and his descendants that the world would belong to him, he did so, not because Abraham obey the law, but because he believed and was accepted as righteous by God. For if what God promises is to be given to those who obey the law, then faith means nothing and God's promise is worthless. The law brings down God's anger; but where there is no law, there is not disobeying of the law. And so the promise was based on faith, in order that the promise should be guaranteed as God's free gift to all Abrahams descendant s –not just to those who obey the law, but also to those who believe as Abraham did. For Abraham is the Spiritual father of us all; as the Scripture says, I have made you father to many nations.

So, the promise is good in the sight of God, in whom Abraham believed—**the God who brings the dead to life and whose command brings into being what did not exist. Abraham believed and hoped, even when there was no reason for**

hoping, and so became the father of many nations. Just as the Scripture says, "your descendants will be as many as the stars". He was then almost one hundred years old; but his faith does not weaken when he thought of his body; which was already practically dead, or of the fact that Sarah could not have children. His faith did not leave him, and he did not doubt God's promise; his faith filled him with power; and he gave praise to God. He was absolutely sure that God would be able to do what he had promised. That is why Abraham through faith, was accepted as righteous by God. The words, he was he was accepted as righteous, were not written for him alone. They were written also for us who are to be accepted as righteous, who believed in him who raised Jesus our Lord from the death. Because of our sins he was given over to die, and he was raised to life in order to put us right with God. Roman 4:13-25

CHAPTER 26

Living by Faith: 2 Corinthians 4:18

For this reason, we never become discouraged. Even though our physical being is gradually decaying, yet our spiritual being is renewed day after day. And this small and temporary trouble we suffer will bring us a tremendous and eternal glory, much greater than the trouble. **For we fix our attention: not on things that are seen, but on the things, that are not seen. What can be seen only last for a time, but what cannot be seen lasts forever. 2 Corinthians 4:18: For** we know that when this tent we live in—our body here on earth—is torn down, God will have a house in heaven for us to live in, a home he himself has made, which will last forever.

And now we sigh, so great is our desire that our home which comes from heaven should be put on over us, by being clothed with it we shall not be without a body. While we live in this earthly rent, we groan with a feeling of oppression, it is not that we want to get rid of our earthly body, but that we want to have the heavenly one put on over us, so that what is mortal will be transformed by life. God is the one who has prepared us for this change, and he gave us his spirit as the guarantee of all that he has in store for us. **So, we are always full of courage.** We know that as long as we are at home with the body we are away from the Lord's home. **For our life is a matter of faith, not of sight. (2 Corinthians 5:7) We are full of courage.**

CHAPTER 27

Be Anxious for Nothing

Do not be anxious for nothing: Do not be anxious for anything but in everything by prayer and supplication and thanksgiving; make your request made known to God, and the peace of God which passed all understanding will keep your mind at rest: This is why I tell you: do not be worried about the food and drink you need in order to stay alive, or about clothes for your body. After, all, isn't the body worth more than clothes? Look at the birds: they do not plant seeds, gather a harvest and put in the barns; yet your father in heaven takes care of them Aren't you worth much more than the birds? Can any of you live a bit longer by worrying about it?

And why worry about clothes? Look how the wild flowers grow: they do not work or make clothes for themselves. But I tell you that not even king Solomon with all his wealth had clothes as beautiful as one of these flowers. It is God who clothes the wild grass—grass that is here today and is gone tomorrow, burned up in the oven. Won't he be all the surer to clothe you? **What little faith you have.** So, do not start worrying: Where will my food comes from? Or drink?

or my clothes? (These are the things the pagans are always concerned about). Your father in heaven knows that you need all these things. **Instead be concerned above everything else with the kingdom of God and with what he requires of you and he will provide you with all these other things.** So, do not worry about tomorrow; it will have enough worries of its own. There is no need to add to the troubles each day brings. Do not be afraid of those who kill the body but cannot afterward do anything worse. I will show you whom to fear: fear God, who, after killing, has the authority to throw into hell. A man in the crowd said to Jesus: Teacher, tell my brother to divide with me the property our father left us. Jesus answered him, friend, who gave me the right to judge or to divide the property between you two? And he went on to say them all, watch out and guard yourself from any type of greed; **because your true life is not made up of the things you own.no matter how rich you may be.** The Jesus told them this parable: There was one rich man who had land which bore good crops. He began to think to himself, I don't have a place to keep all my crops. What can I do? This is what I will do, he told himself; I will tear down my barns and build bigger ones, where I will store the grain and all other goods. Then I will say to myself, Lucky man: You have all the good things you need for many years. Take life easy, eat, drink and enjoy yourself: But God said to him, you fool, this very night you will have to give up your life; and then who will get all these things you have kept for yourself? And Jesus concluded, this is how it is with those who pile up riches for themselves but are not rich in God's sight. Luke 12:4, 13-34.

CHAPTER 28

The Rich Man who Refuse to Give to the Poor

The greedy rich man: As Jesus was starting on his way again, a man ran up, knelt before him, and asks him good teacher, what must I do to receive eternal life? Why do you call me good? Jesus asked him. No one is good except God alone. You know the commandments: Do not commit murder; do not commit adultery; do not steal; do not accuse anyone falsely; do not cheat; respect your father and mother. Teacher the man said, ever since I was young, I have obeyed all these commandments. "Jesus looked straight at him with love and said:

You need only one thing. Go sell all you have and give the money to the poor and you will have riches in heaven; then come and follow me: "when the man heard this, gloom spread all over his face, and he went away very sad, because he was very rich. Jesus looked around his disciples and said to them, how hard it will be for rich people to enter the kingdom of God. The disciples were shocked at these words, but Jesus went on to say, my children, how hard it is to enter into the kingdom of God. It is much harder for a rich person to enter into the kingdom of God than for a Carmel to through the eye of a needle. At this the disciples were completely amazed, and asked one another, who, then, can be saved? Jesus looked straight at them and answered, this is impossible for human beings but not for God; everything is possible with God. Then Peter spoke up, look, we have left everything and followed you. **Yes, Jesus said to them, and I tell you that those who leave home, or brothers, or sisters, or mother or father or children or fields for me and for the gospel will receive much more in this world in this present age. They will receive a hundred times, more houses, brothers, sisters, mothers, children and fields—and persecution as well. And in the age to come they will receive eternal life. Mark 10:17-31**

CHAPTER 29

Jesus Said Have Faith

The importance of faith: Matthew 14:30-31. But when he saw the wind, he was afraid, and beginning to sink he cried out, Lord save me Jesus immediately reached out his hand and took hold of him, saying to him," Oh ye of little faith, why did you doubt? Doubt is about not trusting in someone or believing what someone tells you.

Now faith is the assurance of things hoped for, the conviction of things not seen. The word conviction is the same word used in trying and convicting a criminal of a crime. A conviction comes about by asset of irrefutable facts that convinces a judge or jury to assess a penalty, fine, or imprison someone. The decision is made because of evidence that has been provided.

Ephesians 6:16: Above all, taking the shield of faith, wherewith ye shall be able to quench all the fiery darts of the wicked

And he said to them, why are you afraid, oh ye of little faith?

Then he arose and rebuked the winds and the sea, and there was a great calm. Matthew 8:26

Ephesians 2:8: For by grace you have been saved through faith. And this not your own doing; it is the gift of God.

So, faith comes from hearing, and hearing the word of Christ. Roman 10:17

And without faith it is impossible to please God Hebrew 11:6

But let him ask in faith, nothing wavering. For he that waves is like a wave of the sea driven with the wind and tossed. Don't let your faith wavers when things in life don't go as you planned. James 1:6

Faith without works is dead James 2: 14

Ask, seek knock: Ask, and you will receive; seek, and you will find; knock and the door will be opened to you. For everyone who asks, will receive, and anyone who seeks will find, and the door will be opened to those who knock: Matthew 7:7

Prohibiting and Permitting: And I tell all of you what you bind on earth is bind in heaven, and what you loose on earth is loose in heaven: Matthew 18:18

And I tell you more: Whenever two of you on earth agree about anything you pray for, it will be done for you by my father in heaven. For where two or three come together in my name, I am there with them. Mathew 18:18: The seventy-two men came back in great joy. Lord, they said, even the demons obeyed us when we gave them a command in your name. Jesus answered them, I saw Satan fall like lighting from heaven.

Listen I have given you authority, so that you can walk on snakes and scorpions and overcome all the power of the enemy, and nothing will hurt you. But don't glad because the evil spirits obey you; rather be glad because your names are written in heaven. Luke 10:19. A house or a kingdom divided against himself self shall not stand: When a strong man, with his entire weapon ready, guards his own house, all his belongs are safe. But when a stronger man attacks and defeats him, he carries away all the weapons the owner was depending on and divides up what he stole. Luke 11:17

CHAPTER 30

God's Promises
Received by Faith

Acts Chapter 2 verses 3 and verses1-47

How a true church and the early church operate: Life among the believers: Acts Chapter 2 verses 43-47. Many miracles and wonders were being done through the apostles, and everyone was filled with awe. All the believers continued together in close fellowship and shared their belongings with one another. They would sell their property and possessions, and distributes the money among all, according to what each one needed. Day after day they met as a group in the Temple, and they had their meals together in their homes, eating with glad and humble hearts, praising God, and enjoying the good will of all people. And every day the Lord added to their group those who were being saved.

The believers share their possessions: Acts Chapter 4 verses 32-37: The group of believers was one in mind and heart. None of them said that any of their belongings were their own, but they all shared with one another everything they had. With great power, the apostles gave witness to the resurrection of the Lord Jesus, and God poured rich blessings on them all. There was no one in the group who was in need. Those who own field or houses would sell them, bring the money received from the sale, and turn it over the apostles; and the money was distributed according to needs of the people. And so, it was that Joseph, a Levites born in Cyprus, whom the apostles called Barnabas (which means "One who Encourages"). sold a field he owned, brought the money and turned it over to the apostles

The parable of the great feast: Luke 14: 11-24:

For those who make themselves great will be humbled; and those who humbled themselves will be made great. Then Jesus said to his host, "When you give a lunch or dinner, do not invites your friends or your brothers or your relatives or your rich neighbors—for they will invites you back, and in this way, you will be paid for what you did. When you give a feast, invite the poor, the crippled, the lame, and the blind; and you be blessed, because they are not able to pay you back. God will pay you on the day the good people rise from the death.

When one of the guests sitting at the table heard this, he said to Jesus, "How happy are those who will sit down at the feast in the kingdom of God. Jesus said to him, "There was a man who was giving a great feast, to which he invited many people. When it was time for the feast, he sent his servants to tell his guests, come, everything is ready. But they all began, one after another to make excuses. The first one told the servants, I have bought a field, and must go and look at it.; please accept my apologies. Another one said, I have bought five pairs of oxen, and am on my way to try them out; please accept my apologies. Another one said, I have just got married, and for that reason I cannot come. The servant went back and told all these to his master. The master was furious and said to his servants, hurry out to the streets and alleys of the town, and bring back the poor, the crippled, the blind and the lame: Soon the servants said," Your order has been carried out sir, but there is room for more. So, the master said to the servants, go out to the country roads and lanes and make people come in, so that my house will be full. I tell you all that none of those who were invited will taste my dinner.

Conclusion

HOW TO SURVIVE WHEN YOU LOOSE ALL HOPE IN LIFE IS THE BEST BOOK EVER WRITTEN BY A BEST SELLING AUTHOR BISHOP ISAAC OGBETA TO GIVE YOU HOPE AND STRENGTH FACING CHALLENGES, YOU CAN OVERCOME IS THE GREATEST BOOK EVER WRITTEN TO GIVE YOU HOPE AND THE FAITH AND STRENGTH TO TURN ADVERSITY/ANXIETY/DEPPRESSION INTO OPPOTUINITY/ADVANTAGE

WRITTEN BY
BEST-SELLING AUTHOR
BISHOP ISAAC OGBETA

For more information on how to order copies of this book. "Facing challenges you can overcome": "Turning Adversity/ Anxiety/ Depression into opportunity:" and many other books like "Prayers and Fasting movement": or "Breaking Generation Curses": or Solution to every crises in your life: "etc.: Please contact the Best-Selling Author Bishop Isaac Ogbeta at Cell Phone (347) 502-1065 or visit the websites www.world-widerelieforganization.org

Email: BishopIsaacOgbeta@gmail.com

THE MOST COURAGEOUS AND LOVELY PERSON WHO
EVER LIVED ON THE SURFACE OF THE EARTH IS CALLED
CHARITY THE MARTYR

How to survive when you lost all hope

Believe with conviction brings reality

HOW TO SURVIVE WHEN YOU LOST ALL HOPE

BELIEVE WITH CONVICTION BRINGS REALITY